M

The search for a Northwest Passage from Europe
to Asia led to THE FOUNDING OF AMERICA.

ENGLISH

Cape Cod

DUTCH

Delaware Bay

SWEDES

Connecticut R.

Hudson R.

Delaware R.

Chesapeake Bay

James R.

Cape Hatteras

ENGLISH

Cape Fear

Cape Fear R.

ATLANTIC

OCEAN

FRENCH

SPANISH

SPANISH

St. Lawrence River

L. Ontario

L. Erie

Lake Huron

Chattahoochee R.

Flint R.

Cape San Blas

Lake Superior

Lake Michigan

FRENCH

Alabama R.

Tombigbee R.

Mobile Bay

Lake of
the Woods

Wisconsin R.

Illinois River

Wabash R.

Ohio River

Mississippi River

GULF OF MEXICO

FRENCH

Red R.

Missouri River

Arkansas River

Matagorda
Bay

Red R.

SPANISH

Brazos R.

SPANISH

Pecos R.

Rio Grande

Colorado River

Gila R.

SPANISH

PACIFIC

OCEAN

MAIN AREAS
OF EARLY EXPLORATION
BY EUROPEANS

–·–·– Present-day State boundaries

Scale of Miles

0   100   200   300   400

Map by Harry Scott

A Fresh Look At
AMERICAN HISTORY
Volume 1

The FOUNDING of AMERICA (1492-1763)

G. BRUCE WOODIN

STERLING PUBLISHING CO., INC. NEW YORK

ACKNOWLEDGMENTS

The Author and Publisher wish to thank the following people for their advice and suggestions in regard to this volume and for having oriented the material to the social studies curriculum in the elementary schools, as well as for checking the terminology for easy reading in intermediate grades, beginning at fourth grade level:

Elizabeth Noon
Editor, *The Instructor*

Ada A. Towne
Curriculum Coordinator (Social Studies)
Elementary Schools
Board of Education, City of New York

Lucille Harris
Corrective Reading Teacher
P.S. 132, The Bronx, New York

The Author and the Publisher also wish to thank the staff of the Schomburg Collection of Negro Literature and History of the New York Public Library for their assistance in obtaining information and pictures for this volume.

Indians fought among themselves before and after white men came to America.

Contents

Smithsonian Institution

(Above) Northern Indians chipping stone for arrowheads. The wigwam, made of poles covered with mats, provided protection against cold and rain.

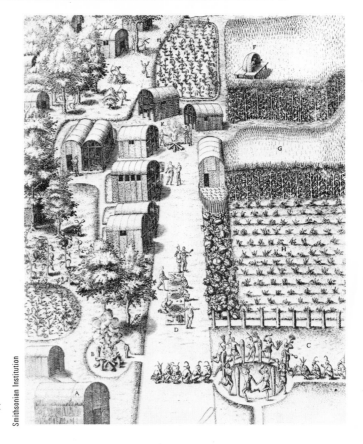

Smithsonian Institution

(Right) Southern Indian village with vegetable gardens. The wigwams, built with rounded roofs, stayed dry during the worst of storms.

Chapter 1

America before the Whites and Blacks Arrived

Where did the first people in America come from? No one really knows. There may have been people in America before the Indians—often called redskins, although their skins were not red. But none of the many legends that have been told have been proved true. New discoveries— ancient skeletons and arrowheads—and new ways of dating these finds, have been making news almost yearly. With these to go by, many historians agree that the Indians who welcomed Christopher Columbus on October 12, 1492, were related to the very first people to live here.

Historians found that the great civilizations the American Indians developed were built entirely on their own. The Aztecs and Mayans in Mexico and the Incas in Peru built temples and monuments of stone as large as the pyramids built in ancient Egypt. Historians know for certain that the Indians spoke many different languages. None of these had any connection with the languages of Asia, Europe, or Africa. Not only that, but their skills and their way of life did much to affect the lives of both white and black people in America later on.

The Indians made excellent jewelry, baskets, pottery, tools, bows and arrows, spears, and canoes. Many of these are treasured today in museums. The Indians showed the white men how to fish, hunt, and live in the forest. From the Indians, they learned how to grow many of our most important vegetable crops — maize (corn), tobacco, potatoes, beans, tomatoes, squash and chocolate, to name a few. White men even learned from the Indians how to bake food in a hole in the ground.

All signs point to Central Asia as the first home of the American Indians. Their physical appearance was very much like that of the Mongolians (Orientals), al-

Indians with boats made of wood and skins. Their village is on the cliff above.

though some Indians in America looked like Europeans. In leaving Asia, the great grand-fathers of the Indians were possibly pressed by enemies from behind. They could very well have made their way across the narrow Bering Strait, between Asia and Alaska, by raft. This may have been toward the end of the Ice Age, about 20,000 years ago. It was at this time that the thick layer of ice that covered most of North America began to melt. Supposedly, other Asians, coming from Siberia, pushed the first arrivals south-ward to the buffalo country of the Great Plains. Then they were pushed into the territory that later became New Mexico and Arizona. There, they became "cliff dwellers," living on the edges of cliffs or in caves. Some, continuing southward, made the dangerous journey to South America, where they spread out over that large continent. The Eskimos, the last to cross the Strait, settled the Arctic region.

These early settlers from Asia brought skills and knowledge with them—language, fire, the art of making flint spear points, and of scraping animal hides for clothing and shelter. Not too surprisingly, they also brought dogs, which they used for hunting, protection, and com-panionship.

How do we know about the early life of the Indians? The answer rests in the discoveries that have been made by arche-ologists, those scientists who spend their lives digging up the earth to uncover and study what was left behind by ancient peoples. The leader of a recent expedition in the Castle Mountains, near Phoenix, Arizona, came upon a cave which showed signs that it had been lived in thousands of years before Columbus came to America.

Other scientists, called geologists, study the history of the earth and its surface, especially as shown by rocks and rock formations. One group, while searching for oil near Midland, Texas, discovered the body of an ancient American Indian woman, who had been buried some 20,000 years ago. In Boston, Massachusetts, workmen, digging the cellar for a modern skyscraper, uncovered a woven fish weir (trap), which was used to catch fish almost 4,000 years ago.

Unfortunately, written language was unknown to the American Indians. All they knew about their past was what they had been told by their grandfathers and storytellers of their tribes. Questioned by early explorers, they could recall only the outstanding happenings of recent years. The idea of working together, the very thing that has made the United States a great nation, was almost unknown to the Indians. The only Indian tribes that ever united were those which lived in what is now upstate New York.

Two chiefs named Deganawidah and Hiawatha (not to be taken for the Indian hero Henry Wadsworth Longfellow wrote about) united the Mohawk, Oneida, Onondaga, Cayuga, and Seneca tribes to form the Iroquois Confederacy, called The Five Nations. The Iroquois, who later became allies of the British against the French, were second to no other Indians north of Mexico. Without question, they ranked with the amazing Aztecs and Incas in ruling their people, in politics, and in military power.

The Indians who lived on the northwest coast of North America at about the time of Columbus's discovery made a fairly

John White painted this picture in 1585, as he watched Indians spearing fish for fun. The Indians used a fish weir (trap) when they made large catches for tribal feedings.

good living for themselves. Mainly, they ate salmon and other fish, which they smoked over fire to preserve for year-round food. They wove baskets and built large dugout canoes. They decorated their dwellings with carved, painted trees, called totem poles, instead of putting name plates outside. Besides this, they owned property, and were so keen at business that they were able to look after themselves in trading with white men.

The Pueblo Indians, who lived in what is now the Southwest of the United States, were great hunters and knew a great deal about farming. They built *adobe* (sun-dried brick) houses, community courts, and buildings in which religious dances and services were held. They also made wonderful baskets, cloth, and pottery. They kept dogs and raised turkeys, hunted with flint-headed spears and bows and arrows, and smoked tobacco in a pipe. They still live today as they did ages ago. The Pueblo Indians provide the best living example of a well-ordered Indian society. The Navajo and Apache Indians learned much from the Pueblos when they first moved into the Southwest during the 16th century.

We know very little about the Indians who lived in the valleys of the Ohio and Mississippi Rivers. This is mainly because they were nomads, or wanderers, and seldom stayed long

New Mexico Department of Development

Sun-dried brick (adobe) houses built by Pueblo Indians. This village, located in New Mexico, can still be seen.

Indian women of a Mound Builders' village mashing sun-dried corn to make cornmeal.

Smithsonian Institution

in one place. Known as the "Mound Builders," they constructed and lived in gigantic, earthen mounds, which looked like huge birds and snakes. They traded with other Indians, tilled the soil with hoes of stone and shell, and painted their bodies a brownish-red color. They were skilled metal workers and even invented a musical instrument, a pipe of bone and copper. As time passed, they gradually disappeared, along with their music, after having buried their dead in tombs as the Egyptians did.

The Indians who lived on the Great Plains, between the Rocky Mountains and the great woodlands which bordered on the Mississippi River, lived partly by raising corn and mostly by hunting buffalo. As if born in the saddle, they tamed and rode spirited mustangs, the offspring of European horses turned

loose by early Spanish explorers. The Indian men, riding their horses, chased and hunted buffalo. The women, who did the heavy work, followed the men

Smithsonian Institution

The Natchez tribe of Great Plains Indians hunted buffalo in this way, first rounding up the herd.

A Great Plains Indian carrying his children on a "travois."

with children and baggage loaded on *travois* (trav-wa), consisting of two poles joined by a frame and drawn by a dog or horse; or, in winter, on toboggan sleds, another Indian invention. The Indians had no wheels. They moved about a great deal, looking for new hunting grounds.

The tribes that lived in what are now Maine and Nova Scotia, southern New England, Delaware, the Middle Atlantic States, Virginia, and the Middle West are the so-called Algonquin language group. This collection of many tribes raised crops and moved around very little. Later the Algonquins saved the first English settlers from starving to death, by providing them with fish, turkeys and other game, baking beans, pumpkins,

and other food. These Indians lived in long, bark-covered houses and were outstanding hunters and fishermen. They invented the birch-bark canoe and the wood-and-rawhide snowshoe. The men went almost naked, even in mid-winter, wearing only short trousers and moccasins made of deerskin. The various tribes produced a number of famous, noble chiefs, such as King Philip, Powhatan, Pontiac, Tammany, and Tecumseh. Some became Christians and adopted white men's ways.

In the southeastern part of North America, the Muskogean Indians—including the Choctaws, Creeks, and Seminoles—were more clearly understood, because their ways were like those of the Europeans. They had a class system: some families lived

(Left) King Philip of the Wampanoag Indians of New England, wearing clothes made of deerskin.

(Below) An educated Mohawk Indian chief, Thayendanegea, who became a Christian and changed his name to Joseph Brant.

like royalty, while the peasants lived like serfs or slaves. They planted corn and made excellent pottery, blankets, and deerskin clothing. The white settlers later taught them how to plant orchards and raise cattle.

(Left) Chief Kickapoo of the Algonquin Indians using a prayer stick as he studies Christianity.

13

A young Indian chief wearing a fancy hairdress, beads, feathers, and furs.

The Indians were far stronger than the Europeans who invaded their land. Although they were finally conquered, the Indians for several centuries lived as they always had, even while white men lived on part of their land.

Things to Remember about Chapter 1

Meanings of Words and Phrases

Continent: One of the seven land masses of the globe; namely, Europe, Asia, Africa, North America, South America, Australia, and Antarctica. Central America, a part of North America, is not a continent.

Historian: An expert in searching old records, telling of past events.

Monuments: A stone, a statue or a building to honor a hero.

Egyptians: The people of ancient Egypt, a country in northern Africa described as "the cradle of civilization."

Mongolians: The people of Mongolia, a region in Asia including China.

Strait: A narrow water passage connecting two large bodies of water.

Europeans: The people of any of the countries of Europe.

Archeologist: A scientist who digs up the earth to uncover and study what was left behind by ancient peoples — relics, monuments, tools, weapons, skeletons, and other things.

Expedition: A group sent out to explore.

Geologist: A scientist who studies the history of the earth and its surface, especially as shown by rocks and rock formations.

Confederacy: A group of tribes or states working together.

Adobe: Sun-dried brick made from a yellow clay, usually found near rivers.

Nomad: A wanderer or person who moves about from place to place, looking for better living conditions and more food.

New World: The western half of the earth (west of Europe), including North and South America and their islands.

Conquered: Overpowered, beaten, crushed.

Check Your Memory

Concerning the various tribes of American Indians . . .

1. What kind of food did they eat? (See pages 7, 10, 11, 12.)

2. What kind of clothing did they wear? (See pages 8, 12, 13, 14.)

3. What kind of shelter did they have? (See pages 6, 8, 10, 11, 12.)

4. What kind of transportation did they have? (See pages 8, 11, 12.)

5. What products did they make? (See pages 7, 13.)

6. What did they do to help the white man? (See pages 7, 12.)

Projects

1. Look at your map and locate the Bering Strait, which the ancestors of the American Indians probably crossed.

2. Using photographic clippings of Asiatic people and American Indians, point out the ways in which they resemble each other, especially in facial features.

3. Using photographs to guide you, make a replica of a typical American Indian village, using toothpicks, cloth, paper, string, glue, paint of different colors,

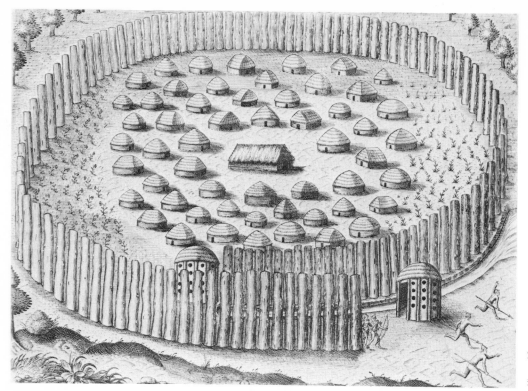

This Florida Indian village is surrounded by a wooden fence for protection against enemies and wild animals.

and small pieces of wood and string to make bows and arrows, wigwams or huts, totem poles, snowshoes, canoes, and spears.

4. Make a mural or drawing showing how a typical American Indian on a reservation lives today.

Coming Up in Chapter 2

The search for an all-water trade route between Europe and Asia . . . Christopher Columbus and the discovery of the New World . . . The Portuguese, Spanish, English, and French explorers.

Questions for Your Classroom Discussions

1. In what ways were the Indians stronger than the white men who first came to America?

2. In what ways could the white man have treated the American Indian more fairly?

3. If you had been born an Indian, what skills would you have learned?

4. Should American Indians today be confined to reservations?

Chapter 2

Early Explorers and Conquerors

Night after night, Christopher Columbus dreamed that one day he would gain wealth and fame for himself. How? He would set sail and discover a new all-water trade route between Europe and Asia. It was all a dream. As it turned out, Columbus discovered something far more important—an island off the coast of an unknown New World.

During the 1400's, Europe had many business problems. The people of Europe were very much in need of a new and better way of trading with people in Asia. Many sharp traders were already trying to do something about it when Columbus was only a lad playing about his father's small wool-combing shop in Genoa, Italy, a seaport on the Mediterranean Sea.

What was in Asia that the Europeans wanted? Products that they could not produce for themselves: sugar, glass, steel,

From "How They Saw the New World"

This is the oldest existing drawing of Christopher Columbus.

and cutlery, which had come from Damascus and Baghdad; rugs, pepper, clove, cinnamon, and nutmeg from Persia, India, and the East Indies; and silk from China. These products they had learned about during the Crusades, a series of wars

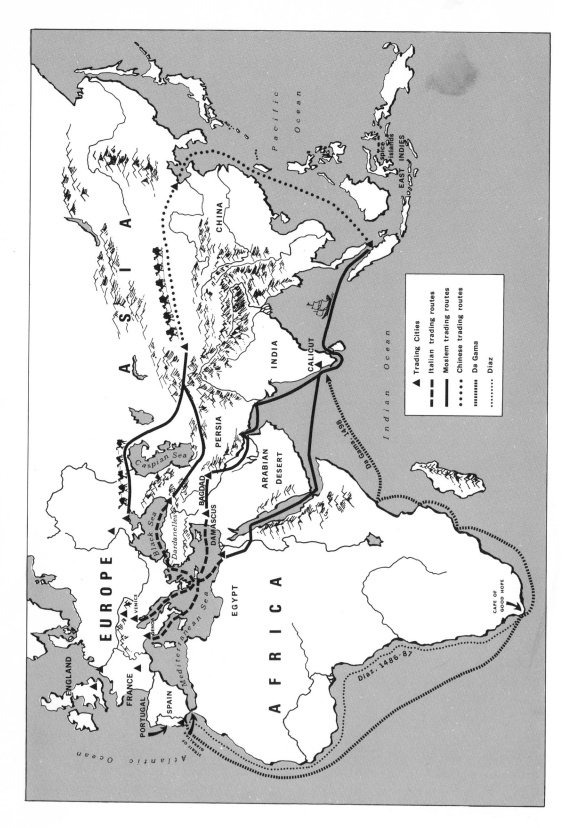

▲ Trading Cities
– – – Italian trading routes
——— Moslem trading routes
•••••• Chinese trading routes
━━━━ Da Gama
•••••••• Diaz

ENGLAND
FRANCE
PORTUGAL
SPAIN
EUROPE
VENICE
GENOA
Mediterranean Sea
Black Sea
Dardanelles
DAMASCUS
BAGDAD
Caspian Sea
PERSIA
ARABIAN DESERT
EGYPT
AFRICA
ASIA
CHINA
INDIA
CALICUT
Spice Islands
EAST INDIES
Pacific Ocean
Indian Ocean
Atlantic Ocean
STRAIT OF GIBRALTAR
CAPE OF GOOD HOPE
Diaz, 1486-87
Da Gama, 1498

18

(1096–1291) fought to regain the Holy Land from the Muslims.

The ancient trade routes were difficult, dangerous, and expensive. It often took months, sometimes years, for a box of spices or a bale of silk to travel from Asia to Europe. Products transported overland from Asia were carried by camel caravans, which had to travel across wide deserts and through mountain passes. Goods moving from the East Indies along the sea-land route had to be shipped across the Indian Ocean and carried over the vast Arabian Desert. Next came another sea voyage across the Mediterranean Sea to the ports of Genoa and Venice.

A famous Italian explorer, Marco Polo, had visited China in the late 1200's, and had come back with wonderful stories and gifts. Since his time, the Italians had made good money from the east-west caravan trade. Now the Portuguese and the Spanish believed that *they* might be able to trade more with the Asians, if they were to discover an easier water route to Asia. Later, the English, the Dutch, and the French thought the same way.

Prince Henry the Navigator of Portugal became the pace-setter. He established a school for seamen and built many ships for them to sail. In addition, he employed the best of Christian and Jewish astronomers and mapmakers, who developed new navigational instruments, including the compass, for finding one's way at sea. Between 1451 and 1470, his sea captains discovered all eight islands of the Azores and colonized them. By 1460, the Portuguese had explored the west coast of Africa and come back with African gold, ivory, and slaves.

In 1488, a Portuguese captain named Bartholomew Diaz made one of the greatest voyages in history, sailing around the Cape of Good Hope, the southern tip of Africa. He would have gone on to India if his crew, tired of being away from home, had not forced him to turn back. Ten years later, in 1498, a fellow Portuguese, Vasco da Gama, followed Diaz's route around the Cape. He completed the long trip across the Indian Ocean, and landed in Calicut, in southern India.

Many great discoveries have been made because of a bold guess. Columbus, guessing that the earth was round, proved it. Disagreeing with other explorers, who thought he was a madman, he headed west! Columbus was an Italian, but it was Queen Isabella of Spain who provided the money for his voyage. Columbus was to keep one-tenth of whatever gold and precious stones he found. So he sailed from Palos, Spain, on August 3, 1492, commanding three little ships—the *Santa Maria*, the *Nina*, and the *Pinta*.

The spot where Columbus landed on the island of San Salvador, in the Bahamas, when he discovered the New World in 1492.

On October 12, 1492, at 2:00 a.m., Rodrigo de Triana, a sailor on the *Pinta*, sighted in the moonlight what turned out to be an island in the Bahamas, which Columbus named San Salvador. Once on shore, Columbus took possession in the name of Spain. The navigator of the *Nina*, a Moor named Pedro Alonzo Nino, became the first black man to land on American soil.

Believing that he was in India, Columbus called the natives Indians. He made three other voyages (1493, 1498, and 1502), discovering a number of other islands in the Caribbean (West Indies). Most important were Puerto Rico (which he called San Juan Bautista), Trinidad, Cuba, Guadeloupe, Antigua, Nevis, St. Croix and some of the other Virgin Islands, and Hispaniola (now containing Haiti and the Dominican Republic). Columbus also sailed along the northern coast of South America, exploring the mouth of the Orinoco River. He died in 1506 without wealth and fame, and without knowing that he had discovered two new continents.

Columbus was followed to America by many other brave men.

Pedro Alvares Cabral, a Portuguese, commanding a fleet of ships heading for India in 1500, got blown off his course by strong winds and landed on the shores of Brazil.

Amerigo Vespucci, an Italian navigator, sailing like Columbus under the flag of Spain, explored the northern coast of South America in 1501. Upon his return to Europe, he wrote a letter in which he said that he had made "a great discovery." "These regions we may rightly call . . . a New World, because our ancestors had no knowledge of them . . . I have found a continent more densely peopled and abounding in animals than our Europe or Asia or Africa," he said.

The news of Vespucci's letter reached geographers who said that the newly discovered land should be called America in honor of Amerigo Vespucci.

There have been other times when places got misnamed, and people failed to get full credit for what they did.

Among the unsung heroes of history were the Vikings. These seamen from the part of northern Europe now known as Scandinavia (Norway, Denmark and Sweden) were sent out in the 6th century to bring back food for their people. They were great shipbuilders and had as many as 700 ships with 40,000 sailors. After invading Ireland and England, they sailed south, in the 9th and 10th centuries,

A Viking ship similar to the one used by Eric the Red and his son, Leif Ericson, when Eric discovered Greenland and when Leif discovered Vinland, in the New World.

around all of Western Europe, capturing ships and looting the coasts. About the year 983, while the Danish Vikings were fighting for control of England, Eric the Red set out with a fleet of swift Viking ships, sailing across the Atlantic to look for new lands. He discovered Greenland. A few years later (about the year 1000), his son, Leif Ericson, sailed his ship from Greenland and discovered a new land, the northeast coast of North America, which he named Vinland. No one knew for centuries that Leif Ericson had found America, for he and his men never returned.

Spain in the 1500's continued to send out explorers and *conquistadors* (conquerors). Vasco Nunez de Balboa was one of them. On an expedition to Central America he crossed the Isthmus of Panama, climbed a mountain, and became the first white man to behold the Pacific Ocean.

In that same year, Ponce de Leon, a Spanish nobleman, sailed along the coast of what he called Florida and paid a visit to the colony he had established in Puerto Rico in 1508. On a later voyage back to Florida, while searching for the Fountain of Youth, a mythical spring, he was killed by an Indian's arrow.

Ferdinand Magellan, a Portuguese, was the first man to sail around the world. In about 1512, while in the Portuguese navy, he sailed around the Cape of Good Hope, fought in India, Malaya, and Java, and went on to the Spice Islands, as the Philippines were then called. This was well into the Pacific Ocean. Then, in 1519, he got his own fleet of ships from the

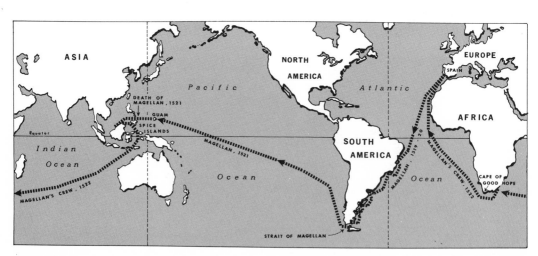

From this map you can see how the first voyage around the world was made. Magellan started out from Spain, went around South America, and crossed the Pacific Ocean to the Spice Islands, where he was killed. His crew then sailed across the Indian Ocean, around Africa, and back to Spain.

Magellan's landing on the island of Cebu in the Spice Islands (later called the Philippines), where he died in battle.

King of Spain and set sail in the other direction.

Across the Atlantic he went, to the southern tip of South America. There he found a windy passage, a short cut, but it took him 38 days to sail through it. It was later named the Strait of Magellan. He had arrived in the Pacific Ocean, but was thousands of miles from his goal. Magellan sailed until he finally reached the island of Cebu in the Philippines, where a war was going on. Here Magellan was killed in battle. But the spot he reached on this west-ward voyage in 1521 was just about as far as he had sailed eastward nine years before. So Magellan was the one who proved without question that the world is round.

His ships went on under a new captain, with Magellan's Malay servant Henriquez on board, around Africa, all the way back to Spain. It was the first complete one-way circle of the globe, and it took three years.

Hernando Cortez, another Spanish *conquistador*, landed on the coast of Mexico in 1519, ready to conquer the wealthy empire of the Aztec Indians and their great leader, Montezuma. He did it by cutting off Mexico City's water supply. He claimed Mexico for the King of Spain, and gained riches for himself.

Until Cortez took Mexico in 1519–21, the Spanish were just establishing trading posts and fringe colonies, or large beach-heads on the edge of the sea. The changeover to Spanish settlements began in Mexico.

Not all of the explorers were successful. Panfilo de Narvaez, who had been poorly treated by Cortez, decided, with high hope of success, that Florida would be his. But, he had hardly set sail from Cuba in 1527 when he lost his two ships in a hurricane. Finding himself somewhere on the west coast of Florida, he made the big mistake of trying to continue his journey, using small boats built by his men. Setting out for the east coast of Florida, he was blown

When Cortez landed in Mexico and fought the Aztecs, he found that they had built pyramids like this a thousand years before he arrived.

in the wrong direction. He sailed
past the mouth of the Mississippi, which he failed to recog-
nize as a river, only to be lost
in a wreck on the coast of
Texas. The four men who survived—Cabeza de Vaca, two
other Spaniards, and a black
man named Estevanico (sometimes called Esteban)—traveled
hundreds of miles overland.
They reached New Mexico and
Arizona; spent six years as
slaves of the Indians; escaped;
and arrived in Mexico City in
1536, after taking the Pacific
Coast route.

Between 1531 and 1535,
Francisco Pizarro, also a Spani-
ard, led an expedition southward
from the Isthmus of Panama to
Peru. Here, high in the Andes
Mountains, he tricked and
murdered Atahualpa, the Inca
Indian emperor, who had been
friendly. Then, with a small
force of men and horses, he
beat down the natives, who
were without a leader but who
fought hard. Pizarro took their
land and made it a colony of
Spain.

In conquering the Aztecs and
Incas, Cortez and Pizarro gave
their country a bad reputation
with the Indians. But Spain, in
control of important parts of
Mexico, Central America, and
South America, was now the
richest, most powerful nation in
the world.

Following the victories of

Pizarro and the 13 men who tricked and
killed Atahualpa, the Inca chief, were
"honored" on this Peru stamp.

their fellow countrymen, other
Spanish *conquistadors* went out
to conquer. Among them were
Hernando de Soto and Francisco
Vasquez de Coronado.

De Soto, who had served
under Pizarro, received a land
grant in Florida from King
Philip II of Spain. Landing at
Tampa Bay, he marched around
in the Gulf area for many
months. He had been told tall
tales about giant cities by men
who had returned from Ponce
de Leon's last expedition. In
1541, de Soto discovered the
Mississippi River and crossed to
its west bank. He spent the
winter in what is now Arkansas,
returned to the river, and died,
wearing golden armor.

Coronado, going northward
from Mexico in 1540, hoped to
find the fabled Seven Cities of
Cibola, whose streets were
supposed to be paved with gold,
and whose buildings were
supposed to be studded with
gems. For months, Coronado led

his men through what is now the Southwest of the United States. One of his lieutenants discovered the Grand Canyon and the Colorado River. Coronado himself marched eastward across Texas, reaching what is now eastern Kansas. Of course,

he never found the Seven Cities of Cibola, nor did anybody else.

England, like Spain, also wanted to claim large areas of the New World. The English port of Bristol, a meeting place for adventurous seamen, was enjoying a profitable trade with

Iceland and the Azores. One day in 1490, there came to Bristol an Italian sea captain named Giovanni Caboto. He wanted to sound like an Englishman, and had changed his name to John Cabot. When King Henry VII had had a chance to back Columbus's first voyage by providing him with money, the king had refused. Now he was sorry. So he was quick to offer John Cabot and his son Sebastian the chance to make two voyages to Newfoundland, Nova Scotia, and New England, in the name of England.

France's claims to a share of the New World were based on the voyages of Giovanni da Verrazano, an Italian free-lance navigator, and Jacques Cartier, a seaman from St. Malo in Brittany, a region in northwestern France.

Verrazano, backed by merchants of Lyon who wanted a shorter route to China's silk, set out in 1524. He tried but could not find a waterway through North America to China. But he was the first European to sail into New York Harbor. The world's largest bridge, which today connects Brooklyn and Staten Island, two parts of New York City, bears his name.

In 1534, Cartier sailed into the Gulf of St. Lawrence, drawing France's attention to this

Cartier explored the St. Lawrence River as far south as Montreal, and made friends with Canada's Huron Indians.

region of Canada. A likable person, he readily made friends with the Huron Indians, who later became very important to France. On his second and third voyages (1535 and 1541), he explored the St. Lawrence River as far south as the present site of Montreal. Along the way, he tried to set up a colony close to where Quebec now stands. The colony failed, but Cartier had done much to start the French in what was later known as New France.

Between 1492 and 1542, all these and other explorers carried the flags of Spain, Portugal, England, and France to the New World. America was still considered by most Europeans as "a sad disappointment."

Things to Remember about Chapter 2

Meanings of Words and Phrases

Trader: A businessman who buys and sells goods or foods.

The Crusades: A series of wars which began in 1096, when the Pope, the head of the Roman Catholic Church, called upon the knights of Europe to get back the Holy Land, which had been taken by the Muslims.

Holy Land: An ancient country in Asia on the coast of the Mediterranean Sea, now divided between Israel and Jordan (Arab Palestine).

Muslim (also Moslem or Mohammedan): People of the religion, law, or civilization of Islam. Their beliefs are based on the teachings of Mohammad, an Arab leader who lived between 570 and 632.

Navigator: A captain who directs or manages a ship on its course, and makes a map of what he discovers.

Moor: A dark-skinned Muslim of the mixed African tribes and Arab people of northwest Africa.

Dense: Thick.

Abounding: Overflowing.

Astronomer: An expert in the science of observation and study of heavenly bodies, such as the moon and the stars.

Compass: An instrument used by navigators or seamen for determining directions — north, south, northeast, for example.

Geographer: One who specializes in the study of the land and physical features of the world, and who makes maps.

Vikings: Pirates from northern Europe (now Scandinavia) who sailed their ships along the coasts of Europe in the 8th to 10th centuries.

Invade: To enter a place in order to conquer it.

Conquistador: A leader in the Spanish conquest of the New World.

Isthmus: A small, narrow piece of land which connects two larger areas.

Establish: To set up on a firm basis.

Colony: A settlement or territory created by a group of people (colonists) who, having left their native land, continue to live under the control of their mother country.

Fringe colony: A large beachhead or area on the edge of the sea.

Check Your Memory

1. Why were the products of Asia so important to Europe? (See page 17.)

2. Why was Europe so interested in an all-water trade route to Asia? (See page 17.)

3. Why were the ancient trade routes so difficult, dangerous, and expensive? (See page 19.)

4. What European nation was the first to become interested in an all-water trade route to Asia? (See page 19.)

5. Why was Columbus called a "madman"? (See page 19.)

Projects

1. Make a copy of the map of the early trade routes between Europe and Asia, which you will find on page 18. Use a red pencil to show which routes were used by camel caravans; a blue pencil to show which were used by sailing ships. Improve or shorten the routes, if you can.

2. Look at the map of the Caribbean and South America on page 26 and locate the areas discovered by Columbus.

3. Trace an outline map of North and South America, using different colored pencils to show the lands explored and claimed by the Spanish, the English, and the French.

4. Read *Westward with American Explorers* by Walter Buehr.

5. Collect postage stamps of different countries—as many as you can—showing pictures of Columbus.

Coming Up in Chapter 3

The Indians and Christianity . . . Slavery . . . The defeat of the Spanish Armada (fleet).

Questions for Your Classroom Discussions

1. If you had gone along on the Crusades to the Holy Land, what would you have brought back from Asia?

2. When would America have been discovered if Europeans had not been looking for a new all-water trade route between Europe and Asia?

3. Was it fair to call the New World America rather than Columbia?

4. In what ways do today's astronauts resemble the explorers of Columbus's time?

Chapter 3

The Spanish in the New World

Within the short space of 50 years, Spain claimed more territory in the New World than Rome conquered in the Old World in 500 years. To gain any real success in controlling this huge empire, Spain had to develop a policy for governing it.

One of the first problems faced by the *conquistadors* was that of dealing with the Indians. The Spanish had always looked down on people outside of Europe as savages, fit for nothing above slavery. Spanish ships seldom sailed past the coast of Africa without stopping to buy blacks from their tribal chiefs or take them by force. Slaves were so common in Spain in 1474 that one of them, a man named Juan de Valladolid, was nominated as "the mayor of Negroes in Seville."

When Columbus returned to Spain in 1493 with Indians and Indian products to show, King Ferdinand and Queen Isabella decided on a new policy. They promised that the Indians in America would be treated kindly and converted quickly to Christianity.

Hispaniola, a large island between Cuba and Puerto Rico, was the first permanent white settlement in the New World (1496). There the native Indians were divided among the colonists, who were told to convert them to Christianity and take care of them. But, as things turned out, Ferdinand's and Isabella's ideas went wrong: the natives were treated as slaves rather than as freemen, and the death rate rose to a new height.

So that Queen Isabella and King Ferdinand could see what Indians looked like, Columbus brought a few back to Spain.

The Spanish galleons had three or four decks, much like Columbus's "Santa Maria." They were used to carry treasure from America to Spain.

Isabella, who was more interested in the souls of the Indians than in their earthly lives, died in 1504. Ferdinand changed his mind about treating the Indians kindly. As a result, everywhere in the Spanish territories, the Indians who were supposed to be *saved*, either became slaves or died. Before long, the colonists were importing black slaves from Africa to do the heavy work, which the Indians would not or could not do, or that the colonists themselves were too proud or lazy to do.

Meanwhile, the Spanish government wasted no time in taking steps to prevent anyone—man or nation—from interfering with its newly-found wealth. All captains of ships sailing from Spain to the New World were to gather information for the King. All American mineral resources—such as gold and silver—were to be set aside for His Majesty's treasury. Certain people were to be allowed to work the mineral-giving lands, but the King was to receive half, or at least one third, of what they got.

The King also owned a fleet of some 60 ships—slow and clumsy, but heavily armed—which sailed back and forth across the Atlantic Ocean. These ships, surrounded by smaller, swifter warships, called the Spanish Armada, left for the Americas with manufactured goods. They returned to Spain loaded with gold, silver, and raw materials, such as mahogany, a wood for making furniture, and flax for making linen. No other country, large or small, was allowed to trade with Spanish America.

The laws for the colonies were made by the King of Spain, who was helped by the so-called Council of the Indies. The Council carefully chose every official to be sent to the New World, and the Council saw to it that all laws were obeyed. American trade was controlled, down to the finest detail, by the

Council and the Official Board of Trade. Only the faithful—the most sincere Roman Catholics—were allowed to leave the country. For, in the New World, no one was to differ with the Church—there were to be no religious "heretics." The Jews and Moors (Muslims) who lived in Spain during this period were now allowed to leave. Since they were not Catholic, they had to serve as slaves, go to prison, or face death. This terrible period (1480–1800) in Europe was called The Inquisition.

In Spain, there were men who were quick to see that there was other wealth, besides gold and silver, to be gained in the American colonies. Some 150,000 people left Spain for the New World in the 1500's, to make homes in Mexico, the West Indies, Central America, and South America, excepting Brazil which belonged to Portugal. Spanish colonists also settled in the southern part of North America; the first settlement was St. Augustine, Florida, founded in 1565. Still another important colony was established in Santa Fe, New Mexico, in 1609. Beyond this, there were many missions and ranches, built by Spanish Catholic priests and others, in California and the southwestern part of the United States.

Most successful of the Spanish missionaries was Father Junipero Serra. In 1750, at the age of 36, he arrived in California to

The Spanish in New Mexico learned to live like the Indians, in pueblo villages.

Father Junipero Serra founded missions all over California and converted the Indians to Christianity. He made his headquarters in Monterey on the Bay of Carmel at the Mission of San Carlos.

convert tribes of nomad Indians to Catholicism. By the time he died 34 years later, he had converted more than 3,000 Indians and instructed them in the arts of peace. Moreover, he had persuaded them to give up their wanderings and settle down to farming. They used the land that surrounded nine missions he had established in Monterey and other places in California.

Agriculture (farming) is the first and most important of all the arts. The colonists who left Spain with farm tools, plants, seeds, poultry, and domestic animals (horses, donkeys, cattle, pigs, sheep, and goats) were highly successful as farmers and ranchers. It was they who actually taught the Indians how to ride horses; before their arrival, the Indians never rode. The settlers grew wheat, barley, rice, sugar cane, lemons, olives, grapes, flax, and other products, many of which were shipped to Spain and sold by traders—at a great profit.

Spanish power reached its highest point in 1580, when King Philip II became the ruler of Portugal as well as Spain. He united two great empires stretching around the world; with his left arm he reached the west coast of Mexico, and with his right arm he touched Manila in the Philippines. The languages and customs of both Spain and Portugal are still highly popular within these "arms."

The Spaniards and the Portuguese built, as we know, rich

King Philip II claimed that he ruled Spain by "divine right."

hand, the sort of rule that we know as the "divine right of kings." Like other rulers before him, King Philip II claimed that God had given him the right to rule Spain, that he was God's representative on earth, and that he was responsible only to God for his actions. The people had little or no say in the government.

While the King depended upon the Council of the Indies for assistance in the management of his colonies in the New World, he also received help from viceroys, or representatives, that he himself appointed and controlled. Each viceroy was given great respect by the colonists, almost as if he were king. Highly important, the viceroy was the King's watchdog, regularly visiting the colonies and checking on their earnings. As an assistant, each viceroy had a captain-general.

To complete the plan, there was a local court, known as the *audiencia*, which was usually made up of three judges who watched over everybody and reported anything suspicious directly to the King.

The King rewarded his loyal friends, nobles, advisers, viceroys, captains-general, and others with rich gifts—gold, silver, land, trading privileges, and the right to operate gold and silver mines.

In "divine right" kingdoms, the government is often ruled by a king's moods. What led to

settlements in the New World. They got gold and silver from the old Indian mines in Mexico, Central America, and South America. They opened seaports wherever possible, and conducted profitable trade between the Old and New Worlds. They printed books, and established schools, missions, and churches. At that time, no other nation in the world had managed to place a single permanent settler on the shores of the Americas.

Never questioned, King Philip II ruled both Spain and the Spanish colonies with an iron

The captains-general appointed by the King lived in Spanish America in great palaces like this.

Spain's loss of power was the weakness of the colonial officials the King now chose. These friends of the King looked for easy money and did foolish things. Instead of building industries in the Americas, they used most of the gold and silver to purchase articles from other countries. The result was that when the flow of gold and silver slowed down, they could neither pay for what they needed nor manufacture it for themselves.

Toward the end of 1580, a heavy gale whipped the waters of the English Channel. Riding the gale into Plymouth, England, came Francis Drake's ship, the *Golden Hind*, returning from a three-year voyage around the world. Its hold was bulging with riches which he had captured from a large Spanish sailing ship, called a galleon.

King Philip, angered by Drake's piracy, demanded that Queen Elizabeth I of England, who had refused his offer of marriage in 1559, behead Drake with her sword to punish him. Instead, the Queen welcomed

Drake as a hero and knighted him, making him Sir Francis Drake. Earlier, she had knighted John Hawkins, the first and most famous English "sea dog" (pirate) and trader in African slaves.

Eight years later, Philip, still angry, sent his Spanish Armada to invade England, only to be thoroughly defeated. To be sure, Spanish power remained strong for many years afterward in both the Old and New Worlds, but Spain after 1588 was no longer the most feared nation in Europe. While Spain became weaker, England, the Netherlands, and France grew stronger.

Things to Remember about Chapter 3

Meanings of Words and Phrases

Old World: The continents of Europe, Asia, and Africa.

Convert: To change faith; also, a person who has been converted.

Policy: A course of action followed by a government, ruler, or political party.

Mineral resources: Gold, silver, iron, copper, and other natural deposits in the earth.

Monopoly: Exclusive control over the supply of goods or services, free from competition.

Heretic: A person who differs with a church, in this case the Roman Catholic Church.

Inquisition: A Roman Catholic court in Europe (1233–1820) and especially in Spain (1480–1800), for the discovery and punishment of "heretics."

Knight: The rank of man-at-arms, serving a king or queen.

Check Your Memory

1. When Columbus returned to Spain in 1493 with Indians and Indian products to exhibit, what promise did King Ferdinand and Queen Isabella make? (See page 30.)

2. Why did the Spanish colonists use black slaves from Africa? (See page 31.)

3. What steps did the Spanish government take to protect its interests in the New World? (See page 31.)

4. What power did the Council of the Indies have? (See page 31.)

5. When was the first Spanish settlement established in North America? Where? (See page 32.)

6. To whom were the viceroys responsible? (See page 34.)

Projects

1. Copy as many Spanish signs as you can find and bring them to class for translation into English. List the goods or services which were of Spanish origin.

2. Ask a Spanish-speaking classmate to teach you the Spanish words for "good morning," "good-by," "please," and "thank you."

Coming Up in Chapter 4

The "Lost Colony" . . . The search for gold . . . Tobacco "madness."

Questions for Your Classroom Discussions

1. What did the Spanish do in North America that still influences your daily life?

2. Do you believe in the "divine right of kings"? Justify your point of view.

3. Do you believe that Spain was right in not allowing Jews and Muslims to settle in America? Give reasons for your answer.

4. What would have happened if the Spanish Armada had defeated the English in 1588?

This carved door gives you an idea of the luxury that surrounded viceroys in Central America.

Chapter 4

The English in the New World

All through the 1500's, England had been as interested as other nations in the New World. Her delay in doing something about the claims that had been made in America by John Cabot was not without reason. To begin with, England was too busy with European problems and was fighting a very long sea war with Spain. Besides, she was faced with troubles at home, arising from religion, politics, and poverty. Yet, toward the end of the 16th century, the necessary planning got done, and England was ready to begin a program of expansion.

Sir Humphrey Gilbert was the Englishman who started it off. Setting sail for America in 1583, he planned to establish a colony in Newfoundland, along the route that he thought was the Northwest Passage to Asia. Unfortunately, Sir Humphrey, along with his crew, was lost at sea.

The following year, Queen Elizabeth I, growing impatient for land in the New World, sent for Sir Humphrey's 31-year-old half-brother, Sir Walter Raleigh, her favorite knight, and asked him to build a colony in America at his own expense. Sir Walter, making the most of his friendship with Queen Elizabeth, managed to get a grant of land that was to include as much of

Queen's Gallery, Buckingham Palace, London

Queen Elizabeth I encouraged her favorite knight, Sir Walter Raleigh, to build a colony in America for England.

North America as England could seize and hold, from sea to sea. In return, Sir Walter decided that whatever territory he opened up would be called Virginia, in honor of Elizabeth, "the virgin queen."

Sir Walter got the extra money that he needed from wealthy Englishmen and sent out an exploring party under Captains Amadas and Barlow. The two captains spent two months exploring the Atlantic coast, off what is now North Carolina. The report that they gave to Sir Walter in England in 1585 was so very good that he organized, under Ralph Lane, a 108-man colonizing expedition.

This group included artist John White, whose picture of an Indian couple appears on the cover of this book; surveyor Thomas Hariot; and a Jewish Bohemian gold prospector named Joachim Ganz. They landed on Roanoke Island, off the coast of the territory that had been looked upon by Amadas and Barlow as a likely location for a colony. The newcomers were somewhat less than happy about the place, and in 1586, when Sir Francis Drake stopped by to see how they were getting on, they all asked for and got passage home.

Sir Walter sent out another group of colonists in 1587, this time 116 in number, for a new try at establishing a permanent colony on Roanoke Island.

In the first colony which Sir Walter (left) founded on Roanoke Island, Virginia Dare (right, in her mother's arms) became the first white child to be born in America.

During that first year, Virginia Dare, the first white child of English parents in America, was born. By the end of the year, new supplies were badly needed, but the shipment was held back by the Spanish Armada's attempt to storm England. When the relief ship finally reached the settlement four years later, the ship's crew searched the island for days, but could find no sign of the settlers. To this day, no one knows what became of this "Lost Colony."

The 16th century (the 1500's) drew to a close without England's having planted a colony in the New World. King James I, succeeding Elizabeth, made peace with Spain in 1604. Now the English, no longer held back by war, moved ahead. King James I issued charters (contracts) to two groups of merchants, allowing them to create two settlements in the New World. One group, operating from Plymouth, England, was known as the Plymouth Company; the other, operating from

The three ships, the "Susan Constant," the "Discovery," and the "Godspeed," brought the first permanent English settlers to Jamestown, Virginia, in 1607.

London, was known as the London Company.

In granting the charters, the King promised that all who settled in the New World would keep their rights and privileges as Englishmen. As we shall see later, the colonists had to remind the English government of this promise, over and over again.

The London Company, with 120 colonists, got the first start. On December 20, 1606, three small ships—the *Susan Constant*, the *Godspeed*, and the *Discovery*—left England to cross the Atlantic Ocean and create a

colony in the New World. The settlement, established in Virginia in the spring of 1607, was called Jamestown, in honor of the King. Captain John Smith, the leader of the colonists, declared that "heaven and earth never agreed better to frame a place for man's habitation." The settlers, reduced by deaths to 104, soon took a different view.

There were many problems in beginning a colony in a wilderness. In fact, if it had not been for Captain Smith's skill in making friends with Powhatan and being assisted by him, the colonists would probably not have survived. Powhatan's daughter, Pocahontas, interested in the settlers, became a Christian and changed her name to Rebecca in 1613.

Captain Smith and all of Jamestown was in a sea of trouble. The location of the colony—a marshy, mosquito-infested island in the middle of a river—could not have been worse. The men refused to dig wells and chose instead to drink the river water. Knowing little or nothing about carpentry work, they built flimsy shelters, in which they were drenched by rain in summer and tortured by cold in winter. In the entire group, there were no more than a dozen skilled workmen; the rest were gentlemen who had

Pocahontas, daughter of the chief Powhatan, saved the life of Captain John Smith and later married John Rolfe.

never done a day's work in their lives.

Yet, not all of the blame for the early failures rested with the settlers. The London Company, back in England, also made a number of mistakes. Reminded of Spain's rich discoveries in the New World, the company's directors demanded that the settlers get busy and look for gold. The settlers were not against the idea—but, unfortunately, there was no gold to be found. The men's time would have been better spent building better houses and growing more crops.

To make things worse, no private property was allowed the settlers, so they had no desire to work. Twice a day, they were marched to the fields or woods

Captain John Smith was the leader of the Jamestown colony.

to the rhythm of a drum, marched back to the settlement, and into church. Whatever they did produce went into the colony's storehouse. They led an almost hopeless life, and there seemed to be no future. The men, made sick by the food that they managed to get from the Indians, caught malaria from mosquitoes in summer and died like flies in autumn. By the end of the year, only 53 were still alive.

The reports of those who made it back to England were so discouraging that King James had to reorganize the London Company with a new charter in 1609, bringing in new blood, money, and a change of system.

Much to the surprise of everybody, it was tobacco that really saved the Virginia colony. The value of the "weed" was discovered by John Rolfe, a Virginian, who had imported seed from the West Indies and crossed it with Virginia's Indian-grown variety. The result was a pipe tobacco which, back in England, became immediately popular. The colony went "tobacco mad," and shortly the whole of Europe was placing orders for "Rolfe's blend." King James, a sensible man in many ways, condemned the smoking habit as "loathsome to the eye, hateful to the nose, harmful to the brain, and dangerous to the lungs." The more the King objected, the more the people

bought tobacco. John Rolfe became very rich and married the former "Miss Pocahontas" in 1614 — the first important "interracial marriage" in America. The couple, not well accepted by Virginia society, were well treated by the English when they visited London in 1616. Their son, Thomas, was educated in England and later returned to Virginia, where he gained fame as a tobacco planter.

It was not too long before there were more than 1,000 white men in the Virginia colony, most of them earning their living by growing tobacco. There were other reasons, too, for the growth of Jamestown. Among the new settlers came many skilled workmen—carpenters, bricklayers, blacksmiths, farmers, and fishermen. Beginning in 1618, the year Sir Walter Raleigh died, each man who paid his own way from England to America was given 50 acres of land. The London Company gave up its colony storehouse; the colonists were allowed to work their own lands and sell their own products.

The directors of the London Company had been thinking that Virginia would attract more colonists if the settlers had some voice in the government. On July 30, 1619, the colonists were given the right to elect 22 burgesses, or representatives—two

Jamestown has been rebuilt as it was in 1607 and can be visited today. This picture shows James Fort with its church, storehouse, guardhouse and homes. The guards are dressed as they were in the 1600's.

from each of the settled districts along the James River. The group, called the House of Burgesses, held a short, but most important, meeting on that day, discussing new laws for "the good of the colony." It was the first step toward democracy in the New World.

The London Company, in that same year, decided that the colony needed the help of the "gentler sex." So it shipped, without delay, 50 women from England to Virginia, all of whom were quickly married. As the

London Company had thought, the women had a steadying effect on the men. Married couples, such as the Dales, the Argalls, and the Smiths, were allowed to build homes for themselves, while the bachelors had to go on living in barracks.

One morning, toward the end of 1619, a Dutch ship landed in Jamestown with 20 Africans, the first of many blacks who would work in and help build America.

The black people who came to the English colonies during

The first women arriving at Jamestown in 1619. Fifty came, all were quickly married, and this had a steadying effect on the whole colony.

these early years were *not* slaves. Like thousands of white people who arrived from Europe, they worked as servants or laborers for a period of years to pay back the cost of their transportation. Once they had repaid the debt, they settled on their own land and worked for themselves. At least one black freeman, Anthony Johnson, had his own slaves.

True, there were Africans being brought to the English colonies in the 1640's—but slavery did not actually take root in Virginia until after 1681. By the end of the 17th century, there were reportedly 3,000 black and 15,000 white servants and laborers, out of a total population of about 75,000.

Even though conditions continued to improve in Virginia, King James, at times hard to please, still believed that the colony could be managed better. In 1624, he took the charter away from the London Company and made Virginia a royal colony. He appointed a royal governor and a 12-man council to help him, but in no way changed the House of Burgesses or the rule of law.

Europe, torn apart by religious struggles, was a terrible place for many people in the 1500's and 1600's. Nearly all Europeans belonged to the

Roman Catholic Church. The trouble began when a group of men in the church started to question some of its practices and beliefs. One of these men was Martin Luther in Germany; another was John Calvin in Switzerland.

These men and others who questioned the Pope's actions finally broke away from the Roman Catholic Church. The Catholics spoke of these "protesters" as Protestants. The Protestants called the movement the Reformation. This religious conflict was a great deal more than a battle of words. Armies marched, wars were fought, and thousands died.

England made her break with the Roman Catholic Church in 1534. King Henry VIII, father of Queen Elizabeth I, who had six wives before he died, argued with the Pope over getting divorces. In anger, the King established the Church of England, also called the Anglican Church. All Englishmen, regardless of their own religious beliefs, were required by law to belong to the King's church and to give money for its support.

In spite of the law, large numbers of Englishmen raised objections to the Church of England. Roman Catholics insisted upon their right to worship as they always had. Among the Protestants were some people, called Dissenters, who felt that the Church of England was too much like the Roman Catholic Church.

One group of Dissenters was willing to belong to the Church of England. But they tried in every way to reform or purify it. These Protestants came to be known as Puritans.

Other Protestant Dissenters refused to have anything to do with the Church of England and broke away to form the Presbyterian, Baptist, Congregational, Methodist, and other Protestant churches. For this reason, they were called Separatists. The Pilgrims belonged to this group.

Life in England was never easy for Dissenters. They were often persecuted by their neighbors, fined by the government, and sent to jail. Believing that they should be free to worship as they pleased, many of them left England for the New World, hoping to find religious freedom.

For a period of more than 100 years, from 1534 to 1642, Englishmen hardly dared to say what they thought on the subject of politics. The problem began to come to a head in the reign of James I. Exercising the "divine right of kings," King James insisted that he was accountable to no one for his actions. When he tried to make and enforce laws without the consent of Parliament, most members of that governing body disagreed with his views on government, but he could do nothing about it. The situation got worse when Charles I became King. While he ruled for 11 years, from 1629 to 1640, Parliament did not meet. Then, in 1642, a civil war, the Puritan Revolution, broke out and did not end until 1649, when the King was beheaded. For the next 11 years, England was ruled by a group of Puritans, with Oliver Cromwell as their leader.

During this period of political confrontation, whoever was in power mistreated those not in power. To escape this, many Englishmen hoped to get political freedom by moving to the New World.

Not all of the people in England's crowded jails were criminals. Many were locked up simply because they could not pay their bills. They remained in jail until their bills were paid— or until they were sent to one

City of Birmingham, England

Oliver Cromwell was the leader of the Puritans in England in a civil war there. He ruled for 11 years and when he was overturned, more Puritans escaped to America.

of the English colonies to work off the money they owed. Many poor people, living no better than slaves, were willing to risk anything to get a fresh start in life.

Things to Remember about Chapter 4

Meanings of Words and Phrases

Surveyor: A person whose work is to survey or measure land.

Prospector: A person who searches and explores the land for minerals.

Charter: An official document granting certain rights, powers, or privileges to a person or group.

Director: One who supervises or directs.

Interracial: Involving members of different races.

Democracy: Government by the people.

Royal colony: A colony ruled by a royal governor and council appointed by the king, and possibly having a representative assembly elected by the people.

Meanings of Words and Phrases

Reformation: A religious movement in the 16th century which urged the reform of the Roman Catholic Church, and which led to the establishment of the Protestant Church.

Church of England (Anglican Church): The national church, Catholic in belief and worship, but independent of the Pope.

Puritan: One of a class of Protestants that arose within the Church of England in the 16th century, demanding reforms in belief and worship.

Pilgrim: One of a class of Protestants that broke away from the Church of England in the 16th century.

Dissenter: One who differs in religious or political opinion and rejects the beliefs and authority of the Establishment.

Parliament: The legislature or Congress of Great Britain.

Check Your Memory

1. Why did England have to wait until the late 1500's to establish claims that had been made in the New World by John Cabot in 1497–98? (See page 38.)

2. What early attempts did England make to establish colonies in the New World? (See pages 38, 39.)

3. What promise did King James I of England make to the colonists when he granted charters to the Plymouth and London Companies? (See pages 40, 41.)

4. Why was the establishment of the Virginia House of Burgesses so important? (See page 43.)

Projects

1. Trace on a map the territory covered by the Virginia land grants.

2. Read *Walter Raleigh* by Henrietta Buckmaster.

3. Using a biography as a reference, write a short article about what happened to Pocahontas.

Coming Up in Chapter 5

The voyage of the *Mayflower* . . . The first Thanksgiving . . . The revolt of the Reverend Roger Williams.

Questions for Your Classroom Discussions

1. What do you think happened to the "Lost Colony"?
2. If you had been at Jamestown, would you have moved the colony to another location? Why?

The "Mayflower" as it looked when it carried the Pilgrims across the Atlantic to Plymouth, Massachusetts, in 1620.

Chapter 5

The Pilgrims and the Puritans in New England

The Pilgrims, filled with hope, set sail from Plymouth, England, on September 16, 1620, heading westward toward the New World. They had planned to land near the mouth of the Hudson River, an area that was then within the boundary of Virginia, and without settlers.

But a great wind, blowing wildly over the Atlantic Ocean, drove their little ship, the *Mayflower*, off its course. On November 11, 1620, when the Pilgrims sighted land, they were looking at a sandy, wind-swept peninsula that would come to be known as Cape Cod.

48

Word spread quickly on the ship that the Pilgrims had no lawful right to be where they were. It was many miles north of the territory held by the London Company. In other words, they were entirely out of bounds in no man's land!

The Pilgrims were worried, but still believed that they had every reason to be thankful. They had successfully crossed an unmapped ocean and arrived safely in the New World. Their original number of 102 had been reduced by only one death at sea.

Some of the Pilgrim leaders, like Captain Miles Standish and William Brewster, announced that they could very well settle in Cape Cod if they wanted to, since no one had the power to tell them what to do. Other Pilgrim leaders, including John Carver and William Bradford, acted quickly to stop such talk of independence. Meeting in the captain's cabin, they wrote up an agreement called the "Mayflower Compact." According to this agreement, all Pilgrims would be free to help shape the government for the new colony. Also, all of them would be expected to obey the laws that they themselves would pass. Elected by the people, John Carver became the colony's first governor.

Library of Congress

The agreement or Compact which was signed aboard the "Mayflower" before it landed set the pace for future documents in American history.

The rock at Plymouth where the Pilgrims landed is surrounded by pillars today and is a favorite spot for visitors.

National Park Service

Thus, only one year after the Virginia House of Burgesses was set up, Englishmen had taken another important step toward self-government in North America.

After having explored and decided that Cape Cod would not make a good spot for a settlement, the Pilgrims moved on, looking for a protected harbor. They soon found one. Captain John Smith had been there before and named the place Plymouth. The *Mayflower* landed here on December 16, 1620, unloading its tired, but hopeful, passengers.

Life was difficult from the very beginning for the Pilgrims, for none of them had ever really learned to rough it. Their crude cabins were little stronger than paper against the hard, bitter New England winter. Only 50 of them survived. However, they never lost their faith, and they had no fear. In the spring, when

the *Mayflower* was readied to return to England, every Pilgrim decided to stay in the colony.

With the help of a kindhearted Indian named Squanto, the Pilgrims learned to grow corn, squash, beans, pumpkins, and other vegetables. Captain Miles Standish, a master rifleman, taught them to shoot wild turkey, deer, rabbits, and other game. Fish, clams, oysters, and lobsters were plentiful. When autumn came, the Pilgrims were anxious to celebrate their harvest and their newly found freedom.

They asked the friendly Wampanoag Indians to share their first feast of Thanksgiving. They also asked Massasoit, the chief of the tribe, to make a treaty with them. Toward the end of the meal, 30 new colonists arrived from England aboard the *Fortune*! Within a matter of days, another ship, the *Speedwell*, landed with Pilgrims who had been living as exiles in Holland.

50

(Right) At Plymouth the logs were sawed like this. One man stood in a pit and the other on a ladder.

Plimoth Plantation, Plymouth, Mass.

(Below) The Pilgrims held their first Thanksgiving in late November, 1621, and invited the Wampanoag Indians who had been friendly with them.

Painting by J. L. G. Ferris, courtesy of William E. Ryder and the Smithsonian Institution

Today, the houses and farmyards of the Pilgrims have been rebuilt for visitors to see. This reconstructed village is called Plimoth Plantation.

By the time that William Bradford succeeded John Carver as governor in 1621, the Pilgrims were producing enough of everything that they needed for themselves. They farmed, fished, and hunted. They even carried on some trade with England, shipping furs, lumber, and dried fish. Yet, in spite of its success,

Snow is falling on the rebuilt homes at Plimoth Plantation as a woman dressed in a costume of the times walks across the yard.

Children, dressed in the costume of the 1620's, play Pilgrim games at Plimoth Plantation.

Plymouth remained small. Some years later, however, in 1691, it became an important part of the much larger Massachusetts Bay Colony.

The Puritans, as we know, had shown a willingness to remain members of the Church of England, if they could bring about reforms. The King, who refused to give an inch, would have none of this. The government took its orders from the King. So, it expelled all Puritans from Oxford and Cambridge Universities in England and

A woman dressed like a Pilgrim is roasting a chicken on a spit in a fireplace at Plimoth Plantation.

53

The life of Massachusetts Bay colonists centered around church activities. The Pilgrims in this painting are going to church on Sunday.

ordered all Puritan clergymen to conform or get out of the Church.

A group of Puritans believed that New England held the answer to their problem. Led by Sir Richard Saltonstall and John Winthrop, they outsmarted the King. They obtained a royal charter, and soon organized the Massachusetts Bay Colony. As good luck would have it, the men who wrote the charter forgot to name the place where the colony's directors were supposed to hold their yearly meetings. By doing this, they protected themselves from the King. Otherwise he could have seized the valuable charter any time he wished.

Making the most of this mistake, the directors voted to take the colony's charter as quickly as possible to New England, where they could be freemen. This had an important influence on future American institutions, since it made the colony almost independent of England.

During the first six months of 1630, some 15 ships, carrying over 1,000 Puritans, sailed from English ports for New England. Ten years later, more than 20,000 people had set up housekeeping in the Massachusetts Bay Colony. These colonists organized into close groups for safety and companionship. They established several settlements—in Shawmut (an Indian name), later called Boston, and in Naumkeag, later called Salem.

The Puritans were not like the

Pilgrims in Plymouth, who had arrived in the New World almost penniless. The Puritans had plenty of food and clothing. In addition, they had tools and other things necessary for building homes. They made money shipping furs and organizing local fisheries. In fact, they found the market for dried codfish so profitable that they made a wooden image of the fish and hung it as a trade-mark at the colony's headquarters in Boston. Next to furs and fish, the main business was raising cattle and vegetables, which they sold to new settlers.

The unhappy Puritans had left England to establish a better way of life in the New World. But they soon forgot their main purpose. They refused to grant settlers who were not Puritans the same religious and political freedom that they wanted for themselves. Only Puritans were allowed to control the government. Only church members in good standing who also owned property were allowed to vote and hold office. It was all too clear; a non-Puritan did not have a chance.

Very different were the views of the Reverend Roger Williams of Salem. Speaking out loudly and clearly against the church and government, he told his congregation that the Indians should be paid for their lands. He wanted every colonist to be allowed to believe, speak, and

Roger Williams was driven from the Massachusetts Bay Colony because he argued too much with the Pilgrims' church. He fled to Rhode Island, where he established a colony that promised religious freedom to everyone, white and Indian alike.

worship as he pleased. Thrown into jail by the leaders of the Massachusetts Bay Colony, Roger Williams was tried on October 9, 1635. He was found guilty of "spreading new and dangerous opinions." He would have been sent back to England if he had not escaped to the woods and joined his friends, the Narragansett Indians. In the spring of 1636, he bought land from the friendly tribe and founded a new settlement at the northern end of Narragansett Bay, which he called Providence.

Other exiles from the Massachusetts Bay Colony, among

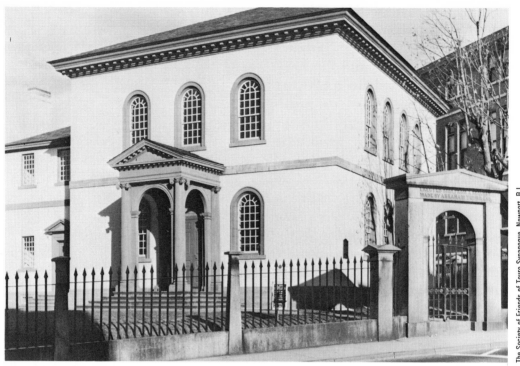

Touro, the first Jewish synagogue in the United States was built in 1762, in Newport, Rhode Island, a colony known for its tolerance. This is the Touro Synagogue as it looks today.

them a woman named Anne Hutchinson, established other colonies along the shores of Narragansett Bay.

One day in 1643, Williams set sail for England. When he came back to New England he had a charter for the colony of Rhode Island which permitted colonists to elect their own governor, rule themselves on local matters, and enjoy religious liberty. Four years later, Williams, helped by other leaders, drew up a plan for a government. This clearly stated that politicians could make laws "only in civil matters." Actually, it meant a separation of church and state (government). Rhode Island, guided by

Roger Williams, became the symbol of religious freedom, not only for America, but for the rest of the world.

Connecticut was another off-shoot of the Massachusetts Bay Colony. The Reverend Thomas Hooker, along with the members of his congregation in Newton, Massachusetts, declared that the time had come to look for a less crowded place. Even in those days, people got the feeling that they were being cramped. In the same year that Roger Williams had bought the land for Providence, the Newton church-men marched cross-country and settled three communities—Hart-ford, Windsor, and Wethersfield. All three were on the Connecticut River, south of the Massachusetts border. A little over 20 years later, in 1662, Connecticut obtained a charter which extended the colony's boundaries to include New Haven and a number of small settlements along Long Island Sound.

Meanwhile, other adventurous colonists from Massachusetts pushed their way northward to settle the towns of Portsmouth, Dover, Exeter, and Hampton. They became the royal colony of New Hampshire in 1679. Others worked their way northeast to what is now Maine, and northwest to what is now Vermont. Strangely enough, Maine and Vermont never became colonies as such. Instead, Maine became a part of Massachusetts, while Vermont was claimed by both New Hampshire and New York.

By the end of the 1750's, the total population of England's continental colonies in America—some of which we have yet to read about—had reached 1,500,000.

Things to Remember about Chapter 5

Meanings of Words and Phrases

Peninsula: A piece of land with water on three sides.

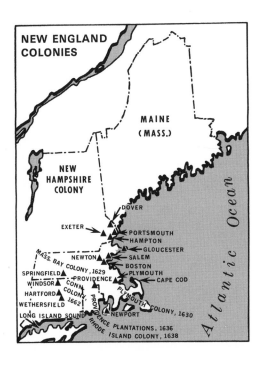

Compact: A written agreement, or contract, between two or more persons, states, etc.

Self-government: Government under the control and direction of the people.

Exile: A person who is banished, or driven, from his home, and forbidden to return.

Trade-mark: A name, symbol, mark, letter, or figure used to identify something.

Civil: Relating to rights of citizens.

State: Depending on how it is used in American history, this word may refer to one of the states of the United States, or to the government of a country or colony.

Migration: Moving from one place to another.

Probably the oldest wooden frame house standing in the United States is Fairbanks House, Dedham, Massachusetts, built about 1637.

National Park Service

Check Your Memory

1. What were the two important points covered by the "Mayflower Compact?" (See page 49.)

2. In what ways did Squanto and Captain Miles Standish help the Pilgrims? (See page 50.)

3. Why did the Puritans disapprove of Roger Williams? (See page 55.)

4. What were the names of the four New England colonies? (See page 57.)

Projects

1. Using your notebook, write up a menu listing the foods which might have been served at the Pilgrim's first Thanksgiving Dinner.

2. Read *The Courage of Sarah Noble* by Alice Dalgliesh.

3. Look at slides of New England today. Compare with Colonial times.

Coming Up in Chapter 6

Manhattan Island is sold . . . The English take New York from the Dutch without a shot being fired!

Questions for Your Classroom Discussions

1. If you had been one of the early colonists, would you have believed in the separation of church and state? Justify your answer.

2. New England became a region of small farming communities. How did geography, religion, trade, and the Indians affect this development?

Chapter 6

Dutch and English in the Middle Colonies

The Dutch lived well in their homes in the Netherlands (Holland) in the 17th century. But they were as anxious as other Europeans to discover a waterway across North America. So they asked Henry Hudson, an adventurous Englishman employed by the Dutch East India Company, to continue the same old search.

It was in 1609, two years after Captain John Smith established Jamestown, Virginia, that Hudson left the Netherlands. He sailed in a ship called the *Half Moon* and headed for America. Arriving in what is now New

Henry Hudson, an Englishman working for the Dutch, sailed up the river later named for him and made friends with the Indians.

Hudson's flagship, the "Half Moon," is honored on this United States coin.

York Harbor, he sailed up the river that has borne his name ever since. He hoped that it would prove to be the Northwest Passage to Asia. But he could go no farther after he reached the rapids north of where Albany, New York, now is. However, he had managed to explore and claim a very important stretch of land, the beautiful Hudson Valley. One year later, in 1610, he discovered in Canada the large body of water which came to be known as Hudson Bay.

Adriaen Block, Cornelius May, and many other Dutch sea captains were eager to fill their ships with furs, and they worked their way up the Hudson River to trade with the Mohawk Indians. Yet no real attempt was made to colonize the area until the Dutch West India Company was organized in 1621. This company, operated by a group of clever Dutchmen, set up trading posts at Fort Orange (Albany, New York) in 1624, and at New Amsterdam (New York City) in 1626. Their man in America, Peter Minuit, bought Manhattan Island—now the cen-

tral section of America's greatest city—from the Manhattan Indians. The price? Some trinkets said to be worth about $24.

The Dutch West India Company wasted no time in taking over the trade along the Middle Atlantic Coast. The Dutchmen completely ignored the charter that King James I of England had given to the London Company. To the Dutch, the legal document was worth no more than the paper it was written on.

In 1629, the Dutch West India Company went all-out to build the colony of New Netherland. Huge areas of land were offered to any member of the company who, within four years, would settle at least 50 tenants on his estate. Besides this valuable

Peter Minuit, as Director General of New Netherland, is the one who purchased Manhattan Island from the Indians.

The Dutch lived in luxury in New Amsterdam. This manor house belonging to the Philipse family has its own water wheel and dock. It has been rebuilt and may be visited today.

prize, the settler would be given hunting and fishing rights, the power to be a judge, and the right to share the fur trade with the company.

Some "company families" were quick to take advantage of this offer. The Van Cortlandts, the Philipses, the Van der Doncks, among others, left the Netherlands to live in America. They soon became powerful land owners, or "patroons." There were also in Holland at the time many "non-company" Europeans, including English Pilgrims and Spanish Jews. They had been living as religious exiles in the Netherlands, and now they wanted to find freedom in America.

Surprisingly enough, most of the Dutch citizens were happy with life as it was in the Netherlands, and had no reason to move to the New World. Few

Dutchmen came to America; the population of New Netherland between 1629 and 1664 never went beyond 10,000.

The settlers, most of whom built and lived in neat gabled houses in New Amsterdam, came from a number of countries. The homes built by the Bownes, the Van Sicklens, and the Wyckoffs may still be seen in Flushing and Brooklyn, New York. In 1646, it was reported that 18 different languages, including Hebrew, could be heard during a walk through the town.

The harbor was always filled with ships, since Long Island Sound and the East River were part of the safest route between New England and Virginia. The Dutch colony, although small, hoped for a healthy, profitable trade in furs. But the Dutch were ruined by the poor judgment of one man—the governor-general of New Netherland, "Peglegged" Peter Stuyvesant.

Stuyvesant had lost a leg while attacking a French fort in the West Indies. He brought much energy to the colony, but little common sense. The rules he set for storekeepers and the high customs duties (taxes) he

"Pegleg" Peter Stuyvesant, governor of the colony, surrendered New Amsterdam to the English in 1664 without allowing a shot to be fired.

New York and its harbor looked like this to the Dutch in the middle 1600's.

put on foreign trade were very harmful to business people. In fact, these rules practically smothered New Amsterdam. He made the Jews pay a special tax, and aroused the anger of Asser Levy, a Jewish immigrant from Brazil. Levy won a court battle, and as a result the tax was withdrawn.

His bad temper and bossy ways angered even the "patroons." In 1655, Stuyvesant, hungry for power, seized New Sweden. This was a weak little colony of Swedish settlers on the Delaware River, which had started in 1638.

In the meantime, the English wanted to occupy all of the coast between Virginia and Massachusetts, so that they could control all the trade. In fact, King Charles II of England planned to take New Netherland and give it to his 30-year-old brother, the Duke of York. So he declared war on the Dutch in America and in Europe.

When the English fleet sailed into New Amsterdam Harbor suddenly in 1664, the Dutch were totally unprepared. Many of the colonists felt little loyalty to the Dutch West India Company and none whatever to the governor-general. So Stuyvesant pulled down the Dutch flag and surrendered without firing a single shot. Thus, in a matter of minutes, the Netherlands lost all of her colonial power in North America.

King Charles II gave the Duke of York the newly-named colony of New York. This was the most valuable grant of land ever made by any English ruler. It included not only the present State of New York, but also the entire region between the Connecticut and Delaware Rivers. Thrown in for good measure were the islands of Nantucket and Martha's Vineyard, and all of Maine east of the Kennebec River.

The Duke of York was generous. He sliced off a large part of his gift—the colony of New Jersey—and gave it to two of his friends, Sir George Carteret and Lord John Berkeley. These gentlemen, also generous, offered large land grants to attract more settlers to their colony from Europe. They also offered religious freedom and a representative government. But they had only limited success. Finally, in 1702, after New Jersey had changed hands many times, the King stepped in and made it a royal colony.

The new colony of New York was quite a mixture of people

Middle Colonies

and races. It included English, Dutch, French, Irish, Swedish, German, Spanish, Italian, and Finnish settlers. All of them added something to the way of life of the colony. The Duke of York tried to be fair. He allowed the conquered Dutchmen to keep their language, religion, customs, and ideas for education. His laws were fairly liberal, based largely on those of the New England colonies. The trouble was that the Duke soon became King James II of England. He never got around to carrying out his good plans. When he was King, he promptly forgot all of them.

In 1686, one year after becoming King, he combined the colonies of New York, New Jersey, and New England. The Dominion of New England was what he called it. He put an end to local government and appointed his own man, Sir Edmund Andros, as governor.

William Penn was greatly admired by the Indians because he made fair deals with them, paid them well for their land, and protected them.

This period of government by a ruler with unlimited power ("arbitrary rule") lasted a little over two years. The English in England were as angry with the King as the English in America were. So they organized a revolt called the Glorious Revolution. They dethroned the King in 1688, and adopted a Bill of Rights. This guaranteed certain basic liberties to every citizen. The new King and Queen, William and Mary, gave the colonies their charters back. The colonial representative assemblies met again.

Meanwhile, William Penn had founded Pennsylvania as a new center of tolerance and religious freedom. Penn was one of the most able governors and the best-loved colonizer in the New World. His wealthy father had been an admiral and a friend of kings. Young Penn had enjoyed an excellent education at Oxford University. In fact, he might have had a brilliant future in the king's service, if he had not decided to visit Ireland in 1667, at the age of 22. It was here that he heard, by chance, a Quaker lecture titled "There is a faith that overcometh the world." Deeply moved by these words, he promptly joined the Quakers, or Society of Friends.

The Quakers were another Puritan group. Living by the commandment, "Thou shalt not kill," they were at this time very unpopular in England, a fighting country. The admiral was disappointed in his son, but still left young Penn a small fortune upon his death. A large part of this was a debt that the Duke of York owed the admiral. Penn sent the Duke a friendly request for the amount that was due. Along with it he asked for a piece of the Duke's enormous New York Colony. In March, 1681, he was given a "proprietorship" over the huge territory that was named for him: Pennsylvania, meaning "Penn's woodland." The charter that he received from the Duke's brother, King Charles II, guaranteed Penn's possession of it. So Penn had almost the same power over his "proprietary colony" as the king had over a royal colony.

Penn knew that his colony had no coastline. So he asked for and got another grant of land to the south, on the west bank of Delaware Bay. This new grant, later named Delaware, was for many years called "the lower counties." Until the American Revolution, both grants stayed in the hands of the Penn family, and were separate colonies.

The Pennsylvania colony which Penn liked to call the "Holy Experiment," offered settlers religious liberty, along with a representative form of government and cheap land. A new arrival could get 50 acres for nothing. And if he had $240, he could buy a 5,000-acre country estate, with a lot in Philadelphia thrown in. A 200-acre farm

The Dutch continued to live well in New York after the English came. This is the Manor House of the Van Cortlandt family, which can be visited today.

could be rented at a penny an acre. Philadelphia, known as the "City of Brotherly Love," was laid out by Penn himself in 1682. The checkerboard layout of the city—a mirror of his tidy Quaker mind—is copied in city planning to this day.

Settlers arrived by the boatload—Quakers from England, Wales, and Ireland; Scotch-Irish Presbyterians; German and Swiss Protestants; and Catholics and Jews from many of the European countries. William Penn kept his promises to everybody, including the Indians.

By the 1750's, the Middle Colonies—New York, New Jersey, Pennsylvania, and Delaware —had become the most successful in the New World. Philadelphia was the largest and busiest seaport; New York City took second place.

Things to Remember about Chapter 6

Meanings of Words and Phrases

Tenant: A person who rents land or a house from a landlord.

Patroon: A person who held a large tract of land granted by the Dutch West India Company.

Arbitrary rule: Government by a ruler with unlimited power.

Guarantee: Official assurance by a government, company or person.

Bill of Rights: A formal statement declaring the people's rights and liberties.

Quaker: A member of the Society of Friends, a religious organization.

Proprietary colony: A colony granted to an individual or group by the British Crown (King), with full rights of self-government.

Customs Duty: A tax collected on the import or export of goods.

Check Your Memory

1. What advantages did a Dutch patroon enjoy? (See pages 60, 61.)

2. Why were the Dutch settlements important to trade? (See page 62.)

3. Why did the King of England want New Netherland? (See page 63.)

4. Why was it so easy for the English to defeat the Dutch? (See pages 63, 64.)

Projects

1. Imagine yourself as a member of the Dutch West India Company. Write an ad or TV commercial to sell Europeans on the idea of settling in New Netherland.

2. Using reference books in

your library, investigate and write a short report on the patroon system in New Netherland.

3. Read a biography of Peter Stuyvesant.

Coming Up in Chapter 7
Lord Baltimore establishes Maryland for Roman Catholics . . . The black code . . . The thirteenth English colony in the New World.

Questions for Your Classroom Discussions

1. Suppose you had lived in William Penn's Pennsylvania. Would you have agreed that the colony was a "Holy Experiment"? State the reasons for your answer.

2. Which one of the Middle Colonies would you have liked to live in? Debate your reasons with someone else's choice.

3. Why did Philadelphia, and not New York City, become the biggest port in the 1750's? How do they compare with each other today?

Chapter 7

The Southern Colonies

Sir George Calvert, the first Lord Baltimore, was a friend of the King of England. So the King cut a generous slice out of northern Virginia in 1632 and gave it to his friend. Lord Baltimore named the area Maryland, honoring the Virgin Mary.

Sir George Calvert was said to be "the most respectable and honest" of the King's men. He had two good reasons for being happy about his colony. First, it would bring him fame and fortune. Second, it would enable him to provide a new home for unhappy Roman Catholics from England and other countries. In return for the land grant, Calvert had to pay the King one-fifth of all gold and silver found in Maryland each year,

The kind of brick house that was built in the South in the 1600's.

National Park Service

The second Lord Baltimore, Cecilius Calvert, with his grandson Cecil and a black servant.

plus two Indian arrowheads. As for government, he had the power to make all laws—provided they were acceptable to both the colonists and the King.

But Sir George Calvert died while the charter for Maryland was being worked out. His son Cecilius, the second Lord Baltimore, became the proprietor of the colony.

Lord Baltimore was as anxious to make money and help Roman Catholics as his father was. He spent most of his bank account fitting out two ships, the *Ark* and the *Dove*. When they sailed out of England in the autumn of 1633, they were under the command of his brother, Leonard Calvert. Much to the surprise of Lord Baltimore, most of the passengers who landed in Maryland were Protestants, and not Roman Catholics. Although Roman Catholics had more problems than Protestants, they were far less willing to leave Europe.

The colony, a pretty town called St. Mary's, was successful from the beginning. It was quick to profit from the mistakes that had been made in Jamestown, Virginia. Large farms, called plantations, spread up and down the banks of bays and rivers, and the owners grew tobacco and vegetables. The waters provided fish, crabs, and oysters.

Oddly enough, Lord Baltimore's profits came from *not* selling land. His lordship offered every new settler 100 acres—free. All he had to do was bring his family and servants from England at his own expense. If the settler brought a woman or child, he got 50 acres more for each. Some settlers were granted as much as 2,000 acres. This was called the "head-right system." Lord Baltimore gained by charging "quit-rents." Although a head-right was free, a tenant either had to pay a small amount of money (a quit-rent) or give service to Lord Baltimore. The yearly quit-rent was less than 50 cents per 100 acres, but it mounted up.

The Protestants outnumbered the Roman Catholics in Maryland. So Lord Baltimore had an act passed, the so-called Toleration Act of 1649. This guaranteed religious freedom to Catholics, in fact to everybody—except Jews and others who did not believe in Jesus Christ.

The first black people who were brought into Maryland and Virginia were slaves for life. But they could become free if they were baptized in the Christian religion. It was church law that only non-religious humans could be made slaves. Just to be sure, the Maryland assembly closed all loopholes. It passed a "black code" in 1664, which made any African in the colony a slave for life simply because of his color. Another law passed in 1671 stated that neither baptism nor being a Christian would free a person from bondage (slavery).

Before this, there were no more slaves in Maryland than in New York or Rhode Island. But after 1700, the number of slaves brought in from Africa increased sharply. By the time of the American Revolution (1776), blacks numbered nearly one-third of the total population.

The remarkable thing was that the English government, which was Protestant, allowed and even encouraged Roman Catholics to live in Maryland. In other colonial empires — Portuguese, Spanish, and French — only Roman Catholics were allowed.

One day in 1663, a group of eight English nobles paid a visit to King Charles II of England. The group included Sir John Colleton and Anthony Ashley Cooper (later Lord Ashley). They were applying for a land grant in Carolina. Their object was to raise tropical items, such as silk and olives. Colonists had hoped to do this in Virginia, but never could. The King, not knowing any more than the nobles did about the climate of Carolina, granted them the Carolina Charter of 1663. This included all lands between Virginia and Spanish Florida. Geography and desires of the settlers gradually divided Carolina into North and South Carolina.

The North Carolina settlers came mostly from Virginia. They built strong cabins, grew their own food, and a "cash crop" of

A group of Cherokee Indian chiefs were brought from the Carolinas to England by a British colonist. There they were entertained by the King, given English clothes, and treated like visiting royalty.

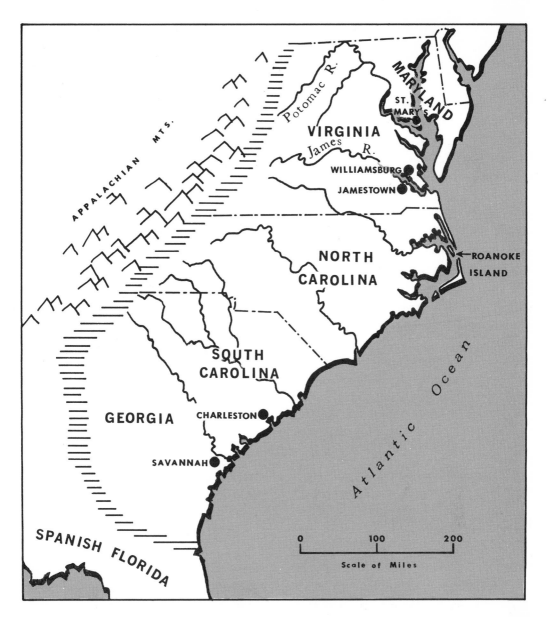

tobacco for shipment to England. Many of them earned their living from the pine forests. They produced lumber and naval stores—tar, pitch, rosin, and turpentine—which they sold to England for her ships.

South Carolina, completely different, attracted more of its settlers from Europe. In and around the seaport of Charles Town (later Charleston), the settlers raised cattle. They also made barrels for export to the West Indies, grew rice, and traded with the Indians for furs. Here, there were Anglican Catholics and Protestants from England; Scots in very large numbers; French Huguenots (Protestants), running from persecution in France; Germans; and emigrants from the West Indies. As time passed, South Carolina also gained large numbers of black slaves. They had to live in shacks, wear white men's cast-off clothing, eat leftovers from white men's tables, and work from dawn to dusk on the plantations.

Both Carolinas were successful from the standpoint of the settlers. But they were unprofitable for the owners of the colonies. In 1729, all but one of the proprietors (Lord Granville) sold out to the King. North Carolina and South Carolina became royal colonies. The same thing happened to almost every other English proprietary colony. The exceptions were those held by the Calverts of Maryland and the Penns of Pennsylvania.

With the founding of Georgia in 1733, England gained her 13th colony in the New World. It was the first sign that England was interested in her southern frontier in America. King George II felt that the English had been all too slow about planting a colony between South Carolina and Spanish Florida. So, he was most anxious to issue a charter for Georgia. A "buffer state" was greatly needed to protect the settled areas to the north, in the event of a Spanish attack.

But General James Edward Oglethorpe, the leader of the group of colonizers, wanted Georgia to be more than just a

On this shingle-horse, a man in the costume of colonial times shows how shingles were made to roof the houses.

barrier to the Spanish. A gentleman of rank and wealth, the General had become an official of the British government and was greatly interested in the poor and unfortunate. In particular, he wanted to help poor debtors. Under the harsh English laws of that time, people who could not pay the money they owed were sent to jail. Oglethorpe wanted to give them a fresh start in the New World.

In 1733, Oglethorpe set up the colony in Savannah with himself as governor. He brought out from England in the ship *Ann* the first load of settlers, 114 in all. The General, wishing to

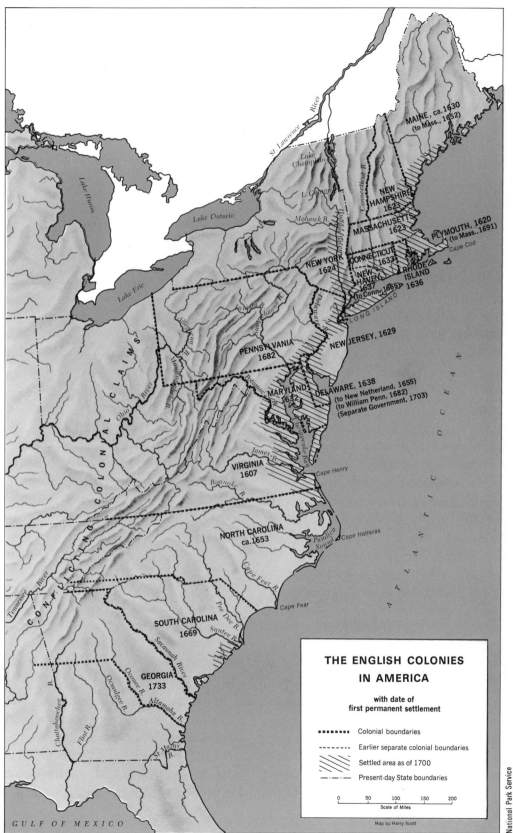

GULF OF MEXICO

THE ENGLISH COLONIES

IN AMERICA

with date of
first permanent settlement

▪▪▪▪▪▪▪ Colonial boundaries

‑ ‑ ‑ ‑ ‑ ‑ Earlier separate colonial boundaries

///// Settled area as of 1700

‑·‑·‑·‑ Present-day State boundaries

| 0 | 50 | 100 | 150 | 200 |

Scale of Miles

Map by Harry Scott

National Park Service

MAINE, ca. 1630
(to Mass., 1652)

NEW
HAMPSHIRE
1623

MASSACHUSETTS
1623

PLYMOUTH, 1620
(to Mass., 1691)

Cape Cod

NEW YORK
1624

CONNECTICUT
1633

NEW
HAVEN
1637
(to Conn., 1655)

RHODE
ISLAND
1636

LONG ISLAND

NEW JERSEY, 1629

PENNSYLVANIA
1682

MARYLAND
1632

DELAWARE, 1638
(to New Netherland, 1655)
(to William Penn, 1682)
(Separate Government, 1703)

VIRGINIA
1607

Cape Henry

NORTH CAROLINA
ca. 1653

Pamlico
Sound

Cape Hatteras

Cape Fear

SOUTH CAROLINA
1669

GEORGIA
1733

CONFLICTING   COLONIAL   CLAIMS

ATLANTIC OCEAN

Lake Huron

Lake Ontario

Lake Erie

St. Lawrence River

Lake
Champlain

L. George

Mohawk R.

Connecticut R.

Juniata R.

Allegheny R.

Ohio River

Potomac R.

James R.

Roanoke R.

Cape Fear R.

Pee Dee R.

Santee R.

Savannah River

Oconee R.

Ocmulgee R.

Altamaha R.

St. Marys R.

Flint R.

Chattahoochee R.

Tennessee River

Chesapeake Bay

A Seminole Indian's "home" in Florida, where the climate is warm and only a roof is needed over one's head.

found a community of small farmers, gave each man 50 acres of land, free and clear. Slavery was banned, and so was the sale of brandy and rum. Land could be left only to male heirs.

But Georgia failed to prosper under the kind leadership of the General. Attempts to attract more settlers resulted in only a small number of immigrants—mostly unhappy New Englanders, Germans, and Scots. Most Georgians were not satisfied with things as they were. They wanted slaves to work for them, and they wanted many more than 50 acres of land, for the growing of cotton, tobacco, peanuts, and other products. Moreover, they did not like the ban on brandy and rum, since it prevented their trading with the West Indies. In time, Oglethorpe had to give in to the demands of the colonists. Georgia became a society of plantations and slaveholders.

Things to Remember about Chapter 7

Meanings of Words and Phrases

Plantation: A large farm or estate in the South, worked by slaves.

Head-right: A grant of land to an individual settler.

Quit-rent: An amount of money paid by a tenant instead of giving service.

Noble: A titled person, such as a duke, lord, or baron.

Bondage: Slavery.

Cash crop: A farm product raised to be sold, not to be eaten or used by the grower.

Huguenot: A French Protestant.

Persecution: Being caused suffering because of one's beliefs or race.

Emigrant and **Immigrant:** A person emigrates from his native land to settle in another. He becomes an immigrant in the country which he goes to.

Buffer state: A small state situated between two larger rival countries. The "buffer" lessens the danger of conflict between them.

British: Native to either England or Great Britain, which consisted of England, Scotland, Wales and (until the 20th century) Ireland.

Check Your Memory

1. Why was Sir George Calvert, the first Lord Baltimore, so anxious to obtain land for the Maryland colony? (See page 69.)

2. What groups of people received no benefit from the Toleration Act of 1649? (See page 71.)

3. What did the "black code," passed by the Maryland assembly in 1664, establish? (See page 71.)

Projects

1. List in your notebook the democratic and undemocratic acts you have discovered in reading about life in the colonies.

2. Dress dolls and prepare an exhibit to show the forms of colonial dress and architecture in Maryland, the Carolinas, and Georgia.

Coming Up in Chapter 8

The French explorers and fur traders . . . Louisiana becomes French.

Questions for Your Classroom Discussions

1. Which city in the 17th and 18th centuries would you have preferred to live in—Boston, New York, Philadelphia, Baltimore, or Charleston—and why?

2. Was Lord Baltimore's Toleration Act of 1649, even with its shortcomings, a liberal development?

3. If you had been a slave in South Carolina, what would you have done about your civil liberties?

4. If you had been in General Oglethorpe's boots, what would you have done to prevent Georgia from failing?

Chapter 8

The French in the New World

During the 1500's, when the Americas were still not fully discovered, France was too busy to think about building colonies. She was trying to conquer Italy and solve problems at home. The voyages that Verrazano and Cartier made for France got little attention. They were seldom talked about. In short, nothing happened until 1608. It was then that Samuel de Champlain set up a permanent trading post at Quebec, in what was called New France.

Toward the end of 1627, Champlain got Cardinal Richelieu, the power behind the French throne, to organize "The Hundred Associates." This was a fur company, and it was to transport some 4,000 settlers, mostly farmers, to the New World within 15 years. The project failed, largely because of religion. Most French Protestants, who wanted to go, were not allowed to leave France. Most French Roman Catholics, who

Samuel de Champlain traveled in Europe and Spanish America before making his first voyage to Canada in 1603. He founded Quebec City and became the first Governor General of Canada.

could leave, were not willing to go. As a result, New France developed slowly.

Quebec had only 70 houses and 550 people in 1660. Of the total population of New France (about 3,500), one-quarter were priests and nuns. As Count

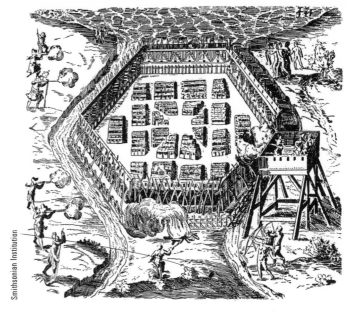

Champlain made this sketch of the Iroquois Indians' fort which he attacked at Onondaga, New York. His allies were the Huron Indians.

Frontenac, one of New France's governors-general, once remarked, "There were but two kinds of business—the conversion of souls and the conversion of beaver."

All plans to grow a surplus of food for export, or to start industries, failed. There was but one cash crop—fur. Beaver pelts were worth one gold dollar each in Quebec and Montreal, the main business centers for fur traders.

Louis XIV, a violent King, used harsh language to voice his opposition to fur trading. The way he saw things in 1661, France needed something more useful than furs. His object was colonization on a grand scale. Moreover, he wanted New France to furnish him with raw materials. These could be converted into finished products and sold at a profit.

Setting out from New France in 1673 were two men: Father Jacques Marquette, a Jesuit missionary, and Louis Joliet, a Canadian-born explorer. Together they crossed the Great Lakes and paddled their light canoes down the Mississippi

La Salle explored the Mississippi River and Valley for France and built Fort St. Louis on the top of Starved Rock, shown here.

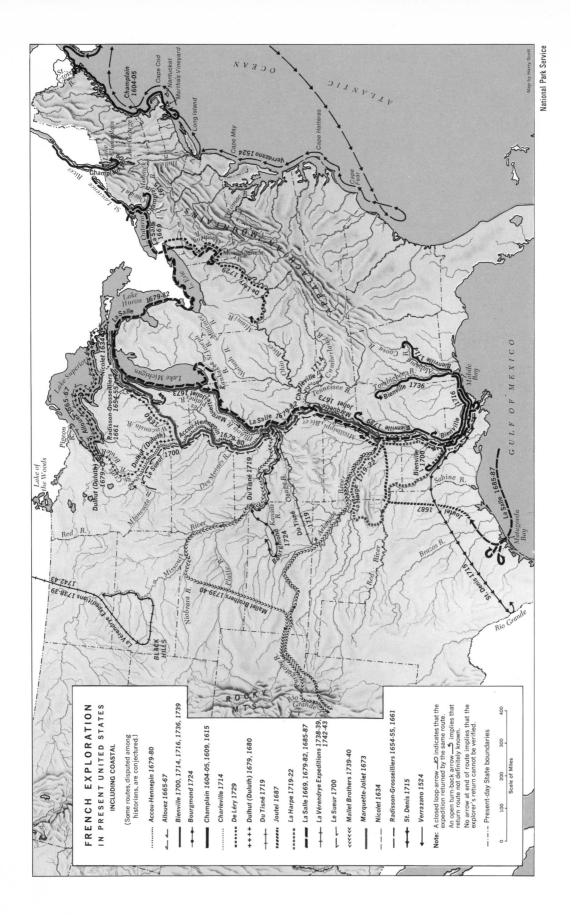

FRENCH EXPLORATION
IN PRESENT UNITED STATES
INCLUDING COASTAL

(Some routes, disputed among
historians, are conjectured.)

Accou-Hennepin 1679-80
Allouez 1665-67
Bienville 1700, 1714, 1716, 1736, 1739
Bourgmond 1724
Champlain 1604-05, 1609, 1615
Charleville 1714
De Léry 1729
Dulhut (Duluth) 1679, 1680
Du Tisné 1719
Joutel 1687
La Harpe 1719-22
La Salle 1669, 1679-82, 1685-87
La Vérendrye Expeditions 1738-39, 1742-43
Le Sueur 1700
Mallet Brothers 1739-40
Marquette-Joliet 1673
Nicolet 1634
Radisson-Grosseilliers 1654-55, 1661
St. Denis 1715
Verrazano 1524

Note: A closed loop-arrow ⟲ indicates that the
expedition returned by the same route.
An open turn-back arrow ↪ implies that
return route not definitely known.
No arrow at end of route implies that the
explorer's return cannot be verified.

––––– Present-day State boundaries

Scale of Miles
0   100   200   300   400

Map by Harry Scott

National Park Service

River to the mouth of the Arkansas River. They had hoped, like so many others before them, to discover a waterway to Asia. Much to their disappointment, they did not find it and were forced to turn back.

Eight years later, Robert Cavalier de la Salle started out with 20 Frenchmen and 30 Indians. They traveled—by canoe and on foot—from Canada to St. Joseph, Michigan. From here they headed for the Mississippi River. Down the explorers paddled, past where the Missouri and Ohio Rivers join the Mississippi. La Salle, who liked people, made friends along the way with many Indians.

In early 1682 they passed the spot where New Orleans would be built. Soon after, the men reached the point where the Mississippi separates into three channels. From here, they made their way to the Gulf of Mexico, where La Salle raised the French flag. He took possession in the name of King Louis XIV. The territory, named Louisiana in honor of the King, included the whole of the Mississippi Valley. It was the largest area ever claimed in the name of a European ruler.

La Salle, in good spirits, returned to Quebec and boarded a ship for France where he reported to Louis XIV. The King first viewed La Salle's trip down the Mississippi River as a waste of time. But, after further thought, he decided to keep hold of Louisiana. He may have had no other reason than to annoy the King of Spain, who was then his favorite enemy.

King Louis XIV reached into the French treasury. He found money enough for La Salle for four ships, a company of soldiers, and an assortment of male and female emigrants.

He also gave the explorer orders to build a fort on the lower Mississippi River. This was in case the Spaniards should decide to make trouble. The expedition, which began in 1684, met with disaster. All four ships overshot the entrance to the Mississippi by 400 miles because La Salle had forgotten to make notes on his map. In need of a port, he landed on the shores of Matagorda Bay, Texas. Then he marched inland, and built a fort near the Garcitas River. Here, on March 18, 1687, the great commander was murdered by his men, who in turn were killed by Comanche Indians.

By the early 1700's, the French had gained control of the two major gateways to the heart of North America. They had fortified settlements in the north at Quebec and Montreal on the St. Lawrence River; and in the south at New Orleans near the mouth of the Mississippi River.

The long St. Lawrence River, flowing between the Great Lakes and the Atlantic Ocean, pro-

The "coureurs de bois" or "runners of the woods" used snowshoes to chase and trap the animals which they sold for their fur. The carefree life attracted more young men to the woods than the towns, and held back the settlement of New France.

vided a natural waterway to the interior of North America. By canoe and "portages" (overland transport of canoes between two bodies of water), explorers and traders could make their way from French Canada to the Mississippi River. The entire plains region between the Appalachian and Rocky Mountains was wide open to the French.

France ranked high in discovery and exploration. She was just as clever as other nations in opening up an empire; was more skillful in handling Indians; and had at least twice the population of England. Yet with all these advantages, she was slow to populate her lands in the New World.

The directors of The Hundred Associates were being pressured by an impatient Louis XIV. So they hit upon what they hoped would be a good plan for New France. In brief, it called for setting up a system of lordships called *seigneuries* (see-nyor-eez). This was somewhat similar to the patroonships of New Netherland. A *seigneur*, according to the plan, could be granted anything from a few acres to 360 square miles of land. In return, he had to guarantee a certain number of *habitants*, or tenants, who would pay a yearly rent and work for him free a certain number of days each year.

This set-up was begun by Louis XIV after New France became a royal colony in 1663. It pleased the *habitants* so well that it even lasted after the English conquest, which took place almost 100 years later. The only ones who objected to it were the fur traders. The trappers, called *coureurs de bois* (coo-roor duh bwa), saw the spread of towns as a threat to both hunting and fur trading.

Fur trading, as it happened, worked in two ways—it strengthened and it also weakened New France. It made money for the trappers, traders, and settlers in New France, and for the shipowners, manufacturers, and bankers in France. But it also kept many of the young men away from home. The carefree life of the *coureurs de bois* attracted far too many of them to the woods. As a result, only a few towns got built and, without towns, New France could not attract new settlers.

At the heart of the colonial system in New France was the governor-general. This one man commanded not only the armed forces, but also all of the departments of government. Under him was a public official known as the *intendant* (ahn-tern-darnt). He really served as spy for the King, keeping him informed on everything that took place.

In addition, New France had a council of about 15 men. This included the governor-general, the *intendant*, the bishop of the church, and at least 12 councilors named by the King. The council, rich in power, issued all decrees, or laws, without asking for the people's vote. Then it acted as the supreme court. Some of the decrees concerned trade between the whites and the Indians. Others concerned the settlers' moral and religious life.

The people who settled in New France looked upon decrees as being almost as bad as

Canada's oldest building is the Jesuit house at Sillery near Quebec City, built in 1637.

imprisonment. Many settlers moved westward to open areas, where they would be free of decrees. New France's population was not so big at this time, and these migrations weakened the colony.

The English colonies, fairly well organized in the 1750's, had certain advantages over their French rivals. For one thing, the English outnumbered the French by 23 to 1. For another, most of the English settlements were confined to a narrow strip of land along the Atlantic Coast. The French were scattered over half the continent.

The English had separate colonial governments, which seldom worked well together, when co-operation was needed. On the other hand, the French were united under a single government and could move quickly when necessary. Besides, the French had the support of many Indians. When the English settlers cleared their land for farms, they drove away the animals which were the Indians' food. The French *coureurs de bois* did not do this.

France, the most powerful European nation in the 1750's, had military forces in Europe ready to help in the colonies when needed.

Things to Remember about Chapter 8

Meanings of Words and Phrases

Trading post: A store in an unsettled region, in which early settlers traded. They exchanged their local products for goods others had made, locally or in the outside world.

Portage: The overland transport of small boats and canoes between two bodies of water.

Populate: To furnish with inhabitants, as by colonization.

Seigneur: A French noble similar to an English lord or a Dutch patroon.

Habitant: A tenant.

Coureur de bois: A trapper, literally "runner of the woods," who traded in furs in New France.

Intendant: A French governor or public official.

Decree: A law.

Check Your Memory

1. Why did the French colonies in North America develop more slowly than the English colonies? (See page 78.)

Check Your Memory

2. Why did "The Hundred Associates" fail? (See page 78.)

3. Why was North American fur trading not only France's greatest strength, but also her greatest weakness? (See page 83.)

Projects

1. Fold a paper in two columns. Head one column "English Colonies" and the other "French Colonies." Find similarities and differences between the two rivals with reference to: (1) type of settlement, (2) type of government, (3) friendship with the Indians, and (4) military strength.

2. Use colored thumbtacks or little paper flags for New France's settlements on the map.

3. Read a story about French Canada and dramatize it in class.

Coming Up in Chapter 9

Major George Washington loses a fight with the French . . . The English and French go to war.

Questions for Your Classroom Discussions

1. Was New France right in spreading over the whole area from Quebec to New Orleans?

2. What ideas would you have suggested in addition to fur trading that would have helped New France to build up her settlements?

Cartier and Champlain are linked
on this Canadian stamp.

Chapter 9

The French versus the English

George Washington was just a boy of 15 in 1747, when Thomas Lee organized the Ohio Company. Lee, heading a group of wealthy Virginians, received from King George II of England a grant of 500,000 acres of land along the Ohio River. He looked upon the area as good for farming. So he planned to carve it up into large plots, which could be sold at a profit. Soon, other Virginians—including Peter Jefferson, Thomas Jefferson's father—formed other companies, and hired traders to get land from the Indians in the Ohio country.

The Marquis Duquesne (pro-nounced Doo-kane), the French governor in Montreal, opposed the Ohio Company's plans. As he saw it, the Virginians were trespassing—entering illegally—in the Ohio country. Not only that, but they were also breaking French communications between Canada and Louisiana. To keep the territory safe, Duquesne sent an armed expedition into the Ohio country.

The Virginians were not easily scared off. In fact, Virginia's governor, Robert Dinwiddie, was quick to act. He sent George Washington, who was now 21 years old, to the Ohio River to warn the French that the land belonged to the English. The warning went the way of the wind. The French refused to move an inch.

Governor Dinwiddie realized that the English would have to face up to a fight. Washington was made a major in the Virginia militia, and was sent with 150 men to stop the French. The French got to the fork of the Ohio River first. They built Fort Duquesne (now

Fort Duquesne, built by the French, was attacked by the British but did not fall. It later became the site of Pittsburgh.

Benjamin Franklin reading proofs for his book, "Poor Richard's Almanack," which included funny sayings and information about weather and crops.

Pittsburgh), and waited to face the Virginia militia. Major Washington fired the first shot, but lost the battle. The French and Indian War was under way.

The French were now settled firmly from the Great Lakes to the Ohio River. They had well-placed outposts throughout the Allegheny Mountains. The entire northern frontier of the English colonies was exposed to attack. On the frontier, the French had their own armed forces, plus Indian allies.

Delegates from seven of the English colonies met to work out a defense plan. They called it a "Plan of Union." Since the meeting was held at Albany, New York, it was called the Albany Congress. There they were joined by Indians of the Iroquois Confederation. The Iro-

quois were the most powerful Indians in North America. Not only were they long-standing enemies of the French, but they were enemies of the Indians who were fighting on the side of New France.

The Plan of Union was largely the work of Benjamin Franklin, a Philadelphia author, scientist, statesman, and inventor. There was to be a president-general appointed by King George II of England. In addition, there was to be a grand council of delegates named by the assemblies of the colonies. The number of delegates was to be in proportion to the money that each colony contributed to the war fund. (This was a typical example of Franklin's foxiness to make certain that local taxes would be paid.) The president, with the advice of the council, was to have the final say in war and peace, Indian affairs, and real estate matters.

The Union would have the power to build forts and organize and finance the fighting forces. It was to operate the treasury and collect money from each colony. The Plan was not popular. Both government officials and settlers feared that they would lose their right to act independently. It was rejected.

One failure led to another. Within a few months, old General Edward Braddock and regiments of red-coated soldiers and officers were sent from

The English sent General Braddock to fight the French and Indians in 1755. His troops moved in straight lines through the woods and were ambushed by the Indians who hid behind trees. Braddock was killed. His colonel, George Washington, saved the British by fighting back Indian-fashion.

England. The "redcoats" were joined by a strong force of Virginians. Together they worked their way, mile after mile, through the Pennsylvania woods toward the French army at Fort Duquesne. The French were waiting in ambush. They attacked suddenly, pouring gunfire into the close-packed British ranks. General Braddock and 63 of his 89 officers were shot dead. The rest, most of them badly wounded, were taken prisoner. The disaster might have been greater. But Major Washington and the Virginia militia fought back, Indian fashion, from the cover of trees and rocks.

General Braddock's defeat was one of the bloodiest in the French and Indian War. It exposed the western parts of Pennsylvania, Maryland, and Virginia to a series of French and Indian raids. Equally important, it gave the Iroquois the idea that the English were going to lose the war. But the English —much to the surprise of everybody—refused to give up. They took defeat after defeat until 1757, when William Pitt became England's prime minister.

Pitt was a lion at leadership. The French and Indian War had grown into a larger war, called the Seven Years' War in Europe.

But Pitt said: "I know that I can save England and that no one else can."

Pitt wasted no time. He fired any official whose only claim to office or rank was birth, wealth, or influence. He worked simply and directly. To the navy, he assigned three jobs: to prevent the French fleet from leaving its home port; to protect English ships carrying troops and supplies; and to operate with the army in sea-to-land operations. The army would be encouraged and strengthened, by having young, strong commanders, such as Jeffrey Amherst, James Wolfe, and John Forbes.

In 1758, General Amherst, together with General Wolfe, took Louisbourg. This was a power-fully armed French fort on Cape Breton Island, Nova Scotia. This victory alone eventually doomed France. It gave the British navy an operating base from which it could cut off troops and supplies coming across the Atlantic Ocean. In the same year, Colonel John Bradstreet, commanding a force of New Englanders, captured Fort Frontenac. This fort was located where the St. Lawrence River flows out of Lake Ontario. This victory weakened French communications to Fort Duquesne. It enabled General Forbes to cross Pennsylvania and take Fort Duquesne, which he renamed Fort Pitt. George Washington was now a colonel on General Forbes's staff.

The French fort at Louisbourg on Cape Breton Island, Nova Scotia. The French had to surrender under a British attack led by Generals James Wolfe and Jeffrey Amherst. It was a turning point in the war, as it allowed the British Navy to get a base on which to land supplies.

The year 1759 was marked by even more sweeping victories for the English. General Amherst, helped by the Iroquois, took over three forts. These were at Crown Point and Ticonderoga, in northern New York, and Fort Niagara, in western New York. The latter was the key fort protecting the entrance to the Great Lakes.

In the same year, General Wolfe brought a large army up the St. Lawrence River. In the early dawn one morning, his men stormed up the cliffs below the Plains of Abraham, just outside Quebec. They quickly took the town from a smaller force under the Marquis de Montcalm, thus gaining control of the St. Lawrence. Both generals were killed in this historic battle. But Wolfe lived long enough to know that he had conquered French Canada for the British.

General of the French Army, the Marquis de Montcalm (shown here), was killed in the Battle of Quebec, and so was the British commander, General Wolfe.

(Below) To win the Battle of Quebec, General Wolfe had to get to the top of the cliff and take the French by surprise. One dark night he led his army across the St. Lawrence River, and under cover of darkness they climbed the cliff. Next morning the French were surrounded.

In September of 1760, after General Amherst had taken Montreal, the French surrendered the whole of New France to Great Britain.

Guadeloupe, a French island in the West Indies, fell to a well-planned English sea-to-land operation. In India, too, French power was smashed by the British. In 1762, two years after King George III took the throne, Spain, fearing a British victory, took sides with France. But her help was both too little and too late.

The Treaty of Paris finally ended the Seven Years' War in 1763.

Great Britain got most of India. More important, she got all of North America east of the Mississippi River, except New Orleans. France was not allowed to keep any of the vast territory claimed by Champlain, La Salle, and others. She got back only a few small islands in the New World—St. Pierre and Miquelon, off the coast of Newfoundland; and Guadeloupe and Martinique, in the West Indies. To pay back her ally, Spain, for her losing Florida to Great Britain, France

Painting by Joseph Blackburn

General Jeffrey Amherst took Montreal from the French. After this, all the French in North America surrendered.

had to give her New Orleans and all of the territory of Louisiana west of the Mississippi River. Napoleon regained this for France in 1800, by defeating Spain in a war in Europe. Cuba and the Philippine Islands, seized by Great Britain in 1762, were returned to Spain.

England and America boiled over with patriotism and loyalty to each other.

Things to Remember about Chapter 9

Meanings of Words and Phrases

Marquis: A nobleman ranking just below a duke and above an earl or count.

Trespassing: The act of entering unlawfully upon the property of another.

Meanings of Words and Phrases

Militia: A body of men enrolled for military service. Militiamen were called out regularly for drill and exercise but served full time only in emergencies.

Outpost: An outlying or frontier settlement.

Frontier: The borderline of a country's settled territory.

Delegate: A person selected to represent others.

Regiment: A military unit consisting of battalions or smaller units.

Regular: In military language, a career soldier.

Ambush: The act of lying concealed, so as to attack by surprise.

Prime minister: The chief executive of a parliamentary government.

Redcoats: British regular army soldiers who wore red coats.

Check Your Memory

1. What started the quarrel between the English and the French in North America? (See page 86.)

2. Who fired the first shot in the battle between the English and the French at Fort Duquesne in 1753? (See page 87.)

3. How much of North America did England get through the Treaty of Paris in 1763? (See page 91.)

Projects

1. Using your map, locate (a) the territory inside and outside of North America, won by Great Britain, and (b) territories given to Spain by the Treaty of Paris of 1763.

2. Suppose you had been one of the representatives of the British government at the Treaty of Paris. List in your notebook the points you would have bargained for in this treaty. What changes would you have made to further Great Britain's interest?

Coming Up in Chapter 10

Acts that helped and hurt the English colonies.

Questions for Your Classroom Discussions

1. Why was Franklin's plan for the Albany Congress "foxy"? Was it a fair plan?

2. How would you compare William Pitt with Winston Churchill, England's great leader in World War II?

3. In what ways did geography influence the military campaigns of the French and Indian War?

The Thirteen Colonies

The British Empire in 1763 might have been called an example of "togetherness." The English, Scots, Welsh, and Irish who had come to America were all loyal subjects. They were happy, for the moment. King George III was supposedly a friend of liberty. William Pitt was widely admired. Both were as popular in America as they were in Great Britain. Surprisingly, things did not work out. The trouble rose largely from what was called the "mercantile system of trade."

According to this system, England tried to obtain and keep more gold than she found necessary to spend. (Every nation wanted to *sell* more goods abroad than it needed to *buy* abroad.) She wanted, in other words, to build a "favorable balance of trade." A nation that could maintain this was not only wealthy, but also powerful.

Colonies were naturally a part of the system. From the English viewpoint, at least, the colonies were expected to provide the raw materials. Without them, the island kingdom, with a growing population, could not supply its own needs. Besides, colonies opened markets for goods produced in Great Britain. They gave the empire added strength,

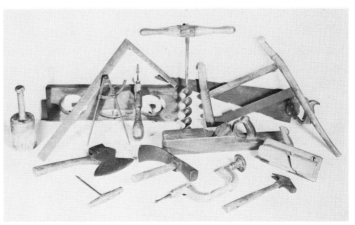

Tools used by colonial workmen in the 1700's. Colonists were allowed to build but could not manufacture. All manufactured articles had to be imported from England.

Colonial Williamsburg

and led to the development of a strong merchant fleet.

The final end of government is not to enforce laws but to do good. The British Parliament ignored this principle. In applying the mercantile system of trade to the colonies, it enacted a number of laws, all of which tended to limit the rights of the colonists.

One series of laws, passed in 1699, limited nearly all manufacturing to Great Britain. They prevented colonists from exporting wool—raw or manufactured—even to a neighboring colony. More laws, passed in 1732 and 1750, made it illegal for colonists to make beaver hats and iron products. The English government was doing everything that it could do to prevent skilled craftsmen from leaving Great Britain. The fear was that colonists would start their own factories.

As early as 1651, another series of laws, known as the "Navigation Acts," were passed. These required all trade between England and her colonies to be carried in British ships. (Most nations, including the United States, apply the same principle today. A French airliner can take passengers from New York City to France, for example, but not from New York City to San Francisco.) This was all right with the colonists as long as their ships were considered British. A powerful merchant fleet, built in the colonies and operated by colonists, was soon sailing the seas. By the time of the American Revolution, some 30 per cent of the British merchant fleet was colony-built.

In 1660 and 1663, other Navigation Acts were passed. These stated quite clearly that trade between the colonies and foreign countries had to be conducted through England. On the export side, the laws named, or "enumerated," certain products, such as tobacco, sugar, cotton, and later, timber and furs. The enumerated products could be exported from colonies *only* to England or to another English colony. The idea was to give the English merchants complete control of these products, which they processed and sold to other countries.

On the import side, colonies could not bring in foreign goods, unless they got them by way of England. Only a few exceptions were made for certain colonial businesses. For example, salt fish from New England could be shipped anywhere. Rice from South Carolina could be exported directly to southern Europe, its main market. In return, the colonies were allowed to import fruit, salt, and wine directly from Spain and Portugal. This idea worked no hardship for the colonies, once they were used to it.

The "enumerated" American products sold well in Britain.

This ironworks, built in the 1600's, made iron bars. It can still be seen at Saugus, Massachusetts.

National Park Service

In fact, they enjoyed a monopoly. The government even paid bounties to certain American producers to encourage the production of certain goods. When the raw materials from America came back from England made into finished products, sometimes the prices were lower than in England. Americans often bought for less than the British.

Thus, the British government followed the mercantile system of trade, as did other colonial powers. As a result, the world was divided into a number of competing empires. This was one of the main causes of colonial wars. In fact, the mercantile system created trouble within the British Empire itself. This was particularly true in its relations with most of the American colonies.

In the beginning, the mercantile system seemed to be especially harmful to the New England and Middle Colonies. All of their products were similar to those produced by British farmers and workers—grain, lumber, fish, cloth, and other items. Out of necessity, these American colonies had to find new markets for their products. Most of this trade was perfectly legal. But some of it was directly against British laws, particularly the Molasses Act of 1733.

The Molasses Act had been proposed and passed in Parliament by friends of plantation owners in the British West Indies. It was intended to force American colonists to buy their much-needed molasses from British planters. However, the planters failed to produce a sufficient quantity of it. So American colonial merchants were almost forced to evade the Act. The British government did not want to make trouble. It decided to follow a policy of ignoring what the colonists were doing. The government was satisfied, as one British statesman, Robert Walpole, expressed it, "to let sleeping dogs lie." So the Act was not actually enforced until 1760.

Generally speaking, British subjects in America—except black people—were the freest people in the world in 1763. True, they argued and fought, not to gain freedom from England, but to preserve what they already had.

In some ways, they were more advanced in governing themselves than Britishers in the mother country—and freer.

Land could pass from one colonist to another without problems. Maximum wages were not fixed as they were in most European countries. Nor were farm workers treated unjustly, as in England and Ireland. Americans were free from compulsory navy service. Military training was required, but actual service, even in time of war, was voluntary. There was almost complete freedom of speech, press, and assembly. Trades and professions were open to the talented. There seemed to be no need for labor unions or special professional organizations. Corporations were not yet thought of. The hand of

government rested lightly. For example, Connecticut went for three years in a row without collecting taxes, except for roads and schools. There were no banks, so merchants loaned money privately. Victory had eliminated the French threat. Attacks by unfriendly Indians would have ended, too, if Americans had stayed east of the Appalachian Mountains.

The thirteen colonies in 1763 contained about 1,500,000 people. One-third of them were black slaves. The Church of England was as popular in the Southern colonies as the Congregational Church was in the New England colonies.

Reviewing the colonies from south to north:

Georgia had forgotten her difficult days. No longer did a General Oglethorpe train New Englanders, Scots, and Germans to fight the Spaniards in Florida. No longer did priests, promising the Kingdom of God, baptize Indians in the Savannah River. Some 10,000 people, including a large number of black slaves, were very much occupied with farming and trade.

South Carolina and North Carolina were very prosperous. Charleston, a gay little town, had a fairly large number of merchants and professional men. It also had a fairly good theater. The wealthy enjoyed life to the full on their elegant plantations. They gave fancy parties and sent

This rebuilt street in Williamsburg, Virginia, shows the home and shop of a successful silversmith. Silversmiths in costumes of the times can be seen today turning out examples of colonial silver.

The Governor of the Colony of Virginia lived in this grand palace built in 1720, considered one of the handsomest buildings in Colonial America. It has ten acres of gardens, including a maze, a canal, a fish pond, and a bowling green. It has been carefully rebuilt and is open for the public to see today.

their sons to Oxford and Cambridge Universities in England. The slaves outnumbered the whites in the Carolinas by two to one. They lived poorly, went without an education, worked 10 to 12 hours a day, and had little or no fun except singing.

In Virginia, there was no such thing as a middle class. A white man was either a "first family" or a rough frontiersman. The upper class was openhanded, liberal, hospitable, and proud of being English. Black slaves had no classes and no liberties, but they accounted for nearly half of the population.

Maryland, with an economy and a social system similar to that of Virginia, depended less on tobacco and more on wheat. Baltimore, a growing seaport, credited its wealth to water power and the manufacture of flour. Annapolis, well-liked by George Washington, was one of the liveliest towns in the Middle Colonies.

In Delaware, some 20 miles from Philadelphia, farms were small but well cultivated.

Philadelphia, the capital of Pennsylvania, was like an average town in England. But it had an added feature: Quaker primness and religion. With over 18,000 people in 1760, it was the largest and most prosperous community in English America.

Going north and crossing the Delaware River by ferry to New Jersey, one would reach Nassau

National Park Service

Philipse Manor in Yonkers, New York, was built by a Dutch family in the 1600's. Later it was used as a village and city hall.

Hall in Princeton, the largest building in the American colonies.

Crossing the mouth of the Hudson River by ferry from Perth Amboy, New Jersey, to New York City, one would find a compact little town, third in population in colonial America. A mixture of people, as it has always been, New York City showed vast differences in wealth. Close to the lovely mansions on Bowling Green were nasty slums, where laborers, stevedores, and free black people lived. Even in 1763, there were enough Irish to celebrate St. Patrick's Day, enough Jews to build a synagogue, enough Scots to support a Presbyterian Church, and enough Germans to maintain four houses of worship.

Up the Hudson River, the Livingston and Van Rensselaer estates covered almost a million acres of land. Four families

99

The Stanley-Whitman House in Farmington, Connecticut, built about 1600, shows the New England style of home and is still standing today.

owned 200 square miles on Long Island. The Stuyvesants and the De Lanceys owned hundreds of acres on Manhattan Island.

New England—that is to say New Hampshire, Massachusetts, Rhode Island, and Connecticut—was largely English, with few blacks, Irish, Scots, or Germans. It was fairly democratic. Almost every adult male had the vote, and great differences in wealth existed only in seaports. Boston, with 17,000 people, was the largest town. Portland (then called Falmouth) exported lumber. Gloucester was famous for fish. Salem traded mostly with the West Indies. Newport, New London, and New Haven were likewise involved in West Indian trade. The wealthiest man in New England in 1763 was Thomas Boylston, a Boston merchant, whose bank account was estimated at $192,000.

Meanwhile, back in England, candles burned late in government offices. British leaders were wrestling with problems arising from the Treaty of Paris of 1763. The big worry was money. The British had fought four costly wars between 1689 and 1763. In the last of these conflicts—the French and Indian and Seven Years' War—the British troops had fought in North America, Europe, Africa, and Asia. Great Britain was

The Pine Tree Shilling was the most famous of the coins used in Colonial Massachusetts. It was coined by John Hull, the official mint-master, who got a percentage of what he coined.

100

deeply in debt. To make things worse, the government needed even more money to maintain the military, so that the empire would be secure. Quite naturally, King George III looked to the American colonists. They were loyal British subjects, and they could help pay part of the bill. In short, taxes in America had to be raised.

The first move in the new colonial program was the Proclamation of 1763. Under this decree, all lands west of the Appalachian Mountains were to become the property of the British Crown. Included, also, was an order directing all settlers in the West to move temporarily to the east of a line drawn along the top of the mountains. This was because of Pontiac's Rebellion, an Indian uprising after the close of the French and Indian War. The idea of the Proclamation was to keep the settlers out of trouble by reserving certain areas of land for the Indians' use.

Also, royal control was extended over the fur trade of the entire West. No fur trader was to enter the region without the approval of British officials.

To the average Britisher in England, the Proclamation seemed quite fair and reasonable. Great Britain had seen, at long last, the need for a regular policy. She had to take a stand on the Indians, the fur trade, and the disposal of Western lands. On the other hand, American fur traders and colonists, who had looked forward to settling in the West, were filled with anger. Angry, too, were the colonial merchants, who had looked forward to making money on the westward movement.

This was only the beginning. There were many more British restrictions yet to come.

Things to Remember about Chapter 10

Meanings of Words and Phrases

Export: To send goods to other countries.

Import: To bring in goods from another country.

Merchant fleet: Ships for trade, as contrasted with a navy fleet for defense.

Beaver hat: A hat, usually a tall stiff hat, made from the fur of a beaver.

Enumerate: To mention items separately, as in counting or in a list.

Bounty: In the sense used in this chapter, a payment made by a government to stimulate the production of certain goods.

Compulsory: Forced.

Voluntary: Not forced.

Stevedore: One who loads or unloads ships in port.

Meanings of Words and Phrases

Economy: What a community or country grows or makes or earns in trade.

First family: A family descended from a colonist or early settler, such as "one of the first families of Virginia."

Democratic: Giving political or social equality to all.

Restriction: An order or law limiting rights and powers.

Check Your Memory

1. What was the main purpose of the mercantile system of trade? (See page 93.)

2. What is meant by a favorble balance of trade? (See page 93.)

3. How did the Navigation Acts cut down on colonial trade? (See page 94.)

Projects

1. Fill in on a time line what you think are the most important events which took place in America between 1492 and 1763.

2. Read *Our Nation's Builders* by Iris Vinton.

Coming Up in "A Fresh Look at American History," Volume 2

Problems in the Empire . . . The Road to Revolution . . . The Declaration of Independence . . . America under Arms . . . The French Alliance . . . A New Kind of Government.

Questions for Your Classroom Discussions

1. Suppose you had been a British colonial official in 1763. What would you have done to sell the colonists on the idea of paying taxes to the British government?

2. If you had been a colonist, what arguments would you have given against paying taxes?

3. What do we have to do today to have a favorable balance of trade?

Index